PICKLEBALL FOR EVERYONE

DISCOVER SIMPLE TECHNIQUES TO QUICKLY MASTER SKILL DEVELOPMENT, BUILD SELF-CONFIDENCE, IMPROVE PHYSICAL FITNESS & INJURY PREVENTION FOR ALL AGES AND ABILITIES

ATWATER PUBLISHING

For Uncle Sam
... and his love for the game.

TABLE OF CONTENTS

INTRODUCTION

Did you know pickleball has transformed from a backyard pastime into a global sensation, captivating participants across every continent in just a few short years? This sport has gained popularity with a staggering increase in courts and a diverse demographic of players. It has become a community where everyone, regardless of age or ability, finds joy and camaraderie.

This book is designed to introduce you to the exciting world of pickleball, whether you're a first-time player or seeking to hone your skills. It's meant for everyone—from curious beginners to seasoned enthusiasts—and it especially embraces players with disabilities, ensuring that the game is accessible and enjoyable for all.

What sets this guide apart is its dedication to adaptive pickleball. While many resources teach the basics, this book dives deep into adaptations and strategies that make the game inclusive. You'll find expert insights and practical strategies, forming a unique blend of content that appeals to a broad audience but with specific, actionable advice.

Structured to ease your journey, the book lays out a clear path from the fundamentals of the game through advanced tactics. Each chapter builds upon the last, offering technical advice, strategic depth, and tips on community engagement. This isn't just about playing pickleball; it's about joining a growing family of enthusiasts who share a love for the game.

As we move forward, we invite you to enthusiastically embrace the pickleball lifestyle. The benefits of this sport extend far beyond physical health, enriching your life with joy and a sense of achievement. This book is more than a guide; it's a gateway to new friendships and endless fun.

So, please take this as your personal invitation to step onto the court with us. Whether you're looking to improve your game or simply searching for a fun way to stay active, let this book be your companion on a fulfilling pickleball adventure. Together, let's explore the excitement and inclusivity of pickleball. Let the games begin!

MASTERING THE BASICS

Did you know pickleball was invented on a lazy summer afternoon in 1965 when three dads, Joel Pritchard, Bill Bell, and Barney McCallum, were trying to entertain their bored families? They improvised using ping-pong paddles, a wiffle ball, and a badminton net, creating a game that is now a phenomenon worldwide. From this humble beginning, the sport has blossomed into a game enjoyed by millions, proving that simplicity can be the ultimate sophistication. As you step into the world of pickleball, remember that everyone starts somewhere, and every champion was once a beginner. This chapter will ensure you grasp the fundamental rules and scoring mechanics, setting you up to play with confidence and enjoyment right from the start.

1.1 SCORING AND RULES FOR BEGINNERS

Understanding how to score in pickleball is your first step towards enjoying this exciting sport. Unlike many other racket sports, only the serving team can score points. Here's how it works: games are played to 11 points, with the winning team needing at least a 2-point lead to secure the victory. To serve, you must announce the score, which always starts with your team's score first, followed by the opponent's score.. The position of the server—the left or right side of the court—depends on whether the score is even or odd. For instance, if your team has an even number, you serve from the right side, and if it's odd, from the left.

The non-volley zone, or "kitchen," is a crucial area on the pickleball court. It's the 7 foot zone on either side of the net where you're prohibited from volleying the ball, meaning hitting it before it bounces. You may step into the kitchen to play a ball that bounces in this area, but stepping on the line during a volley is a fault. It's a unique rule designed to prevent players from dominating the net play, which keeps the game fair and fun.

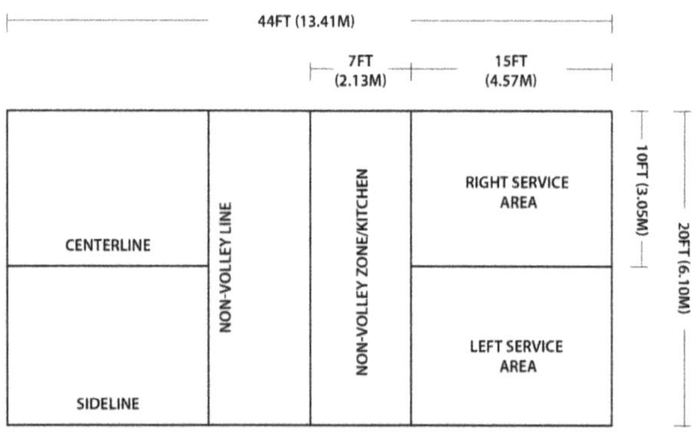

Another fundamental rule is the 'continuous play' principle, which states that the game is designed to flow without pauses. Once the ball is served, players should return it without letting it bounce more than once on their side of the court, keeping the game moving quickly.

Understanding the Serve

The serve in pickleball adheres to the two-bounce rule, which means volleys are not permitted until the ball has bounced once on each side of the net. This rule prolongs rallies and makes the gameplay more strategic. Serving diagonally is a must in pickleball, where you serve the ball crosscourt to the opponent's service box on the other side of the net. It is considered a fault if the ball does not land in the appropriate service box.

Faults and Violations

Common faults include foot faults, service faults, and non-volley zone faults. A foot fault occurs if your foot enters the non-volley zone during a volley or if you step on the baseline or beyond before hitting a service. To avoid this, practice serving behind the baseline, ensuring your feet are correctly positioned before you start your serve. Service faults happen if the ball fails to clear the net, hits outside the opponent's diagonal service box, or if the server makes an illegal serve. Regular practice and awareness of the service rules can help minimize these errors. Lastly, non-volley zone faults occur if you volley the ball while standing in the non-volley zone. Remember, you can enter this zone to play a ball that bounces, but for volleys, you must ensure you are entirely out of the zone, including not touching the line.

By understanding and adhering to these basic rules and scoring systems, you're well on your way to not just playing but thriving in the game of pickleball. Each point you play builds your experience, turning the rules from something you must remember into second nature as you move around the court. So, keep these guidelines in mind, and enjoy every moment on the court!

1.2 CHOOSE YOUR FIRST PADDLE

Selecting the right pickleball paddle can feel like finding the perfect pair of shoes; it's essential to get it just right because your choice can significantly affect your comfort and performance on the court. Let's break down the key aspects when choosing your first paddle, focusing on material, weight, size, grip, and the balance between price and quality.

When it comes to materials, paddles come in a variety of options, each offering different benefits. The most common materials you'll encounter are wood, composite, and graphite. Starting with wooden paddles, these are typically the most affordable and durable, making them an excellent choice for schools, community centers, or anyone on a tight budget. However, they tend to be heavier, which can be a drawback if you play for extended periods. On the other hand, composite paddles are a blend of materials that include fiberglass and polymer, which offer a good balance between weight and durability. They provide a larger variety of weights and handle shapes, which can be a significant advantage as you refine your playing style. While often the most expensive, graphite paddles are lightweight and incredibly responsive, giving you excellent control and power. The graphite surface also provides a better feel for the ball, which helps improve your precision.

Now, let's talk about weight and size. The weight of your paddle is crucial because it impacts your ability to swing and control the paddle throughout the game. Paddles generally weigh between 6 to 14 ounces. A lighter paddle enhances maneuverability and is easier on the arm and shoulder, reducing fatigue and the risk of injuries. However, it might provide less power than a heavier paddle.

Conversely, a heavier paddle can increase your power and drive the ball more effectively but might also lead to quicker arm fatigue. The size of the paddle also matters. While the overall dimensions are somewhat standardized, the hitting surface's size and the handle's length can vary. A longer handle can be beneficial if you have a two-handed backhand, while a wider body might provide a larger sweet spot for hitting.

Grip size is another critical factor. Picking the right grip size contributes to comfort and prevents injuries such as tennis elbow. The grip size should match your hand for optimal feel and control. Hold the paddle with your dominant hand, using a handshake grip to test whether a grip size fits you. You should be able to fit the index finger of your opposite hand snugly in the space between your fingers and the heel of your hand. If there's too much space, the grip is too big; if there's no space, the grip is too small. Most paddles have a grip circumference of 4 to 4 ½ inches, accommodating most players.

Lastly, balancing the cost with quality is important, especially for beginners. While it's tempting to choose the least expensive option when you're just starting, investing more in a mid-range composite or graphite paddle can significantly enhance your playing experience. These paddles offer better feel, control, and durability than most basic wooden paddles. However, if you're unsure about your long-term interest in the sport or are still exploring your playing style, starting with a more economical option might be wise until you're ready to commit to a more advanced paddle.

Choosing the right paddle is a personal decision that can influence your enjoyment of the game. Take your time to try different paddles, consult with more experienced players, and consider how each feels in your hand. Remember, the right paddle for you feels comfortable, suits your playing style, and meets your physical needs on the court.

1.3 ESSENTIAL GEAR

Like any sport, pickleball requires more than just skill and knowledge of the rules; it also demands the right gear to ensure safety, comfort, and optimal performance. Beginning with shoes, the importance of choosing the right pair cannot be overstressed. Imagine playing on different court surfaces; each type has its demands. For example, playing on a concrete surface differs from playing on a wooden gym floor. The right shoes can significantly impact your game by enhancing your movements and reducing the risk of injuries. Shoes designed specifically for pickleball or similar sports typically offer better support and have tread patterns that cater to the quick lateral and forward movements common in pickleball. They also help maintain balance and provide cushioning that absorbs impacts, which is crucial in preventing joint stresses. When selecting shoes, look for those with non-marking soles to avoid leaving scuffs and marks on indoor court surfaces. Also, ensure they have sufficient arch support and are the right fit—not too tight, not too loose—to avoid blisters and discomfort during games.

Choosing the right ball for your playing conditions is crucial. The difference between indoor and outdoor pickleball balls is something that every player should understand. Indoor balls are typically softer and lighter, designed to respond well to indoor courts' smoother, less abrasive surfaces. They have larger holes that allow them to fly slower, making them easier to hit but also requiring more force to get them across the net. Outdoor balls, on the other hand, are made to endure the harsher, rougher surfaces of outdoor courts. They are harder, heavier, and have smaller, more tightly spaced holes, making them less susceptible to wind interference and capable of faster speeds.

Clothing is another critical aspect of your pickleball gear. The proper attire can make a noticeable difference in how comfortably you play, especially during longer sessions or extreme weather conditions. Look for clothes that offer flexibility and do not restrict your movement. Materials that wick moisture away from the body and promote quick drying are ideal, as they help regulate your body temperature and keep you comfortable, regardless of whether you are playing in hot or cool conditions. Shorts, skirts, and shirts with breathable fabrics are most players' go-to choices. They combine functionality and comfort, allowing you to focus entirely on your game without distraction from discomfort caused by inappropriate clothing.

Lastly, don't underestimate the importance of additional accessories like hats, sunglasses, and knee pads. A good sports hat can shield your eyes from the sun, reducing glare and helping you see the ball better. Sunglasses designed for sports use can further enhance visibility on sunny days and protect your eyes from UV rays. Knee pads, while not used by all players, offer added protection, especially for those who dive or fall frequently during play. Each piece of equipment, while seemingly minor, plays an essential role in preparing you for the best pickleball experience possible.

As you assemble your pickleball gear, consider each item a tool to enhance your game. The right shoes, ball, clothing, and accessories can transform your play, making the game more enjoyable and helping you perform at your best. Remember, in pickleball, as in any sport, preparation is vital. Equipped with the right gear, you're all set to hit the court with confidence, ready to meet whatever challenges your opponents throw your way.

TECHNIQUES AND SKILLS DEVELOPMENT

As you dip your toes into the engaging waters of pickleball, mastering the art of serving is like learning to cast a fishing line—the first step to securing your success throughout the game. The serve sets the tone for each point and can be a strategic tool, not just a way to begin play. This chapter will guide you through perfecting your serve, from the basic stance to advanced serving techniques. Understanding and practicing these will boost your confidence and enhance your ability to control the game right from the serve.

2.1 ART OF THE SERVE

Proper Serving Stance and Grip

How you stand and hold your paddle can greatly influence the power and accuracy of your serve. To start, your feet should be shoulder-width apart, with one foot slightly ahead of the other to maintain balance. This stance provides stability and flexibility, allowing you to lean into the serve without losing balance. Your body should be relaxed but poised, with your weight on the balls of your feet, ready to move in any direction once the ball is played.

The grip on your pickleball paddle also plays a crucial role. A firm yet relaxed grip is ideal. Hold the paddle with a shake-hand grip, similar to a firm handshake—tight enough to control the paddle during the swing but loose enough to avoid tension in your arm and wrist, which can lead to fatigue or injury. The V formed by your thumb and index finger should align with the paddle's edge, providing a natural racket orientation for greater accuracy.

Serve Types and When to Use Them

Now, let's discuss the types of serves you can use to keep your opponents on their toes. The power serve is all about speed and force. It drives the ball deep into your opponent's court, ideally pushing them back to the baseline. Use this serve when you want to assert dominance early in the point, especially if your opponent struggles with fast returns.

The soft serve, on the other hand, is subtler and less about brute force. It's about placement and finesse, aiming to land the ball close to the net in the opponent's service box. This type of serve is perfect when facing a strong baseline player—it pulls them forward, forcing them out of their comfort zone.

Lastly, the lob serve arcs the ball high and deep into the opponent's court, giving you time to set up your next move while they deal with the high bounce. It's particularly effective when your opponent is playing too close to the net, as it pushes them back, opening up the court for your next shot.

Practice Drills for Consistency

Consistency is vital in making your serve a reliable part of your game. One effective drill is the target practice serve. To execute, place targets in different areas of the opponent's service box—perhaps a towel or a brightly colored cone. Practice hitting each target with all types of serves, focusing on control and gradually increasing your power as you improve.

Another helpful exercise is the serve repetition drill. Serve continuously for a set number of serves, aiming to get every serve in. Start with ten serves, then increase the number as your stamina and skill improve. This drill builds muscle memory and helps you understand the rhythm and pace of successful serving.

Focusing on these essential elements will transform your serve from a mere game starter to a strategic weapon in your pickleball arsenal. Whether through power, finesse, or cunning placements, mastering the art of the serve puts you in command, dictating the pace and flow right from the first swing.

2.2 HOW TO DEVELOP YOUR BASELINE GAME

When you're standing at the baseline in pickleball, you're not just at the back of the court but at the helm of your ship, navigating the waters of offensive and defensive plays. The baseline isn't just about returning the ball; it's about setting up your next move, controlling the pace, and keeping your opponent guessing. Let's dive into the nuances of groundstroke techniques that make all this possible. For starters, the forehand and backhand groundstrokes are your bread and butter from the baseline. With the right technique, these strokes become powerful tools in your arsenal.

For a solid forehand, position your feet shoulder-width apart, with your dominant foot slightly back and your body side-on to the net. This stance gives you stability and the ability to rotate your hips and shoulders into the shot, generating more power. When you swing, think of it as a smooth, continuous motion. Start with the paddle back, swing forward with your hips leading, and follow through over your opposite shoulder. The follow-through is as crucial as the swing because it dictates the ball's trajectory and spin.

The backhand requires a bit more finesse. Mirror the forehand stance but reverse the foot positioning. Keep your grip firm yet relaxed during the swing, and ensure your paddle face stays perpendicular to the net through the contact point. This will help you maintain control over the direction and height of your shots, which is crucial when you're aiming for specific areas in the opponent's court.

Groundstrokes aren't just about power. They're about placement and strategy. Use these shots to set up offensive opportunities or as defensive tools to neutralize your opponent's attacks. Playing a deep ball keeps your opponent at the back of their court, giving you time to set up your next shot. Conversely, a well-placed angle shot can pull your opponent wide, opening up the court. The pace of your shots plays a significant role, too. A fast, deep shot can push your opponent back, while a slower, well-placed shot might draw them forward, disrupting their rhythm.

Now, let's talk about some common pitfalls. One typical error is poor body alignment; your shoulders and hips should always be aligned with the direction you're aiming the ball. Misalignment can send your shot veering off to the side, making it easy for your opponent to capitalize on the mistake. Another frequent issue is the incorrect paddle angle at the point of contact, often leading to the ball sailing too high or plowing into the net. Lastly, timing mishaps can disrupt your whole game. You must hit the ball early enough to maintain accuracy and power.

To self-correct during games, keep these visual cues in mind:

1. Adjust your paddle angle slightly downward if your shots are consistently going too long.
2. If they're hitting the net, adjust your paddle angle slightly up.
3. Always watch the ball as it hits your paddle to improve timing, and remember, practice makes perfect.

To hone these skills, try some targeted drills:

1. Set up cones at various depths and angles on the other side of the net, and practice hitting them with both forehand and backhand groundstrokes. Start without much power, focusing on accuracy, and gradually increase your pace.
2. Move laterally along the baseline, hitting forehand and backhand shots on the move. This improves your

stroke technique and footwork, vital for getting into the correct position to make the shot.

By dedicating time to these practices, you'll find your baseline game becomes a formidable part of your pickleball play, allowing you to control the court and dictate pace more effectively. Whether setting up a winning shot or fending off a tough rally, these groundstroke techniques and strategies will serve you well, game after game.

2.3 MASTER THE VOLLEY: BASICS TO ADVANCED SKILLS

A volley in pickleball — striking the ball before it bounces — is about quick, snappy decisions and even faster execution. To start, developing a solid volley begins with your paddle always ready, held in front of you, and slightly tilted forward, ensuring you're prepared to meet the ball in mid-air. The essence of good volleying lies not just in your ability to hit the ball, but in how swiftly and effectively you react to it. Your reaction time, a blend of anticipation and reflex, determines whether your volley is just a return or a strategic move that sets you up for winning the point.

Volleying is more about controlled movements than power. It's about precision and placement, manipulating the ball's trajectory and speed to outmaneuver your opponent. When playing at the net, your movements should be sharp and minimal. Overreaching or large, sweeping motions can throw off your balance and timing, making it difficult to recover for the next shot. Instead, keep your feet about hip-width apart for stability, and use small, shuffle steps to adjust your position. This stance helps maintain balance and keeps you agile and ready to move in any direction.

As you grow more confident at the net, you should experiment with some advanced volley techniques. The punch volley, for example, involves a firm forward thrust of the paddle. You will need to give the ball enough speed and direction to challenge your opponent's reaction time.

It's most effective when you aim it deep into the opponent's court or at their feet, forcing them to hit a weak return.

Then there's the block volley, more about using the opponent's power against them. Here, you stiffen your wrist and block the ball, reducing its momentum so it drops neatly over the net. This move can be particularly disarming if your opponent is on the offensive, expecting a harder return.

The swing volley, a more aggressive technique, involves hitting the ball with a short, fast swing.

Use it primarily when adding speed to a high incoming ball or to turn a defensive moment into an offensive opportunity.

It is crucial to position yourself optimally during these exchanges. Ideal volley positioning isn't just about being close to the net; it's about being smart about your placement in relation to the ball and your opponent. Moving strategically towards the non-volley zone line without stepping into it allows you to cover the court effectively and hit volleys with precision. This forward positioning puts pressure on your opponent, reducing their reaction time and opening up the court for you to exploit with your shots.

To sharpen these skills, incorporate drills that enhance hand-eye coordination, reflexes, and paddle control. A great drill to start with involves rapid volley exchanges with a partner, where the goal is not just to keep the ball going but to place your shots accurately under pressure. You can also set up a volley target practice, where areas of the court are marked as targets. The objective is to hit these targets with your volleys, focusing on speed and placement. Another effective exercise is the 'volley ladder' drill, where you and a partner volley continuously while moving laterally along the non-volley zone line. This improves your shot accuracy, footwork, and positioning, crucial elements in mastering the volley.

Through these practices, your volleying skills will evolve from mere reactions to strategic moves that command the net play. Whether you're stopping a hard-hitter with a deft block volley or aggressively taking control with a punch volley, your game at the net will reflect a deeper understanding and a sharper execution, making every volley count.

2.4 THE DINK: NET GAME STRATEGY

In the fast-paced world of pickleball, mastering the dink shot can be a game-changer, especially when the rally heats up, and you're vying for control near the net. Think of the dink as a conversation starter—it's a soft, controlled hit that lands in the opponent's non-volley zone, and it's all about finesse and strategic placement rather than power. This gentle arc forces your opponent to respond in kind, often pulling them out of position and setting the stage for you to make a more aggressive follow-up shot. It's a pivotal move that can shift the game's momentum, making it a critical skill in your pickleball toolkit.

Executing a proper dink requires precision and a gentle touch. Start by positioning yourself close to the net within your non-volley zone, also known as the kitchen. Your body should be relaxed, with knees slightly bent to give you a stable base. Hold your paddle in front of you with both hands for better control, ensuring it's angled slightly upwards to lift the ball over the net. The key to a successful dink is in the softness of your hands—your grip should be gentle, allowing the paddle to cradle the ball rather than propel it. When you strike, use a minimal paddle movement, just enough to guide the ball softly into the opponent's kitchen. The point of contact is crucial; aim to hit the ball at the top of its bounce, which gives you the best angle and highest level of control to place it precisely where you want it.

Dinking becomes particularly advantageous in several strategic scenarios. If your opponent is positioned deep in their court, a well-placed dink can draw them forward, disrupting their rhythm and forcing them to hit a weak return. Similarly, if an opponent shows difficulty handling soft shots, consistent dinking can exploit this weakness, keeping them off-balance and unable to launch powerful returns. By varying the placement of your dinks—sometimes aiming straight ahead and other times angling them towards the sides—, you can keep your opponent guessing and moving, which might lead to errors on their part or create openings for you to exploit with more potent shots.

Incorporating specific drills into your practice sessions can be incredibly beneficial to refine your dinking technique. One effective exercise is the crosscourt dink challenge. Here, you and a partner or coach stand diagonally across from each other at opposite non-volley zones. The goal is to exchange dinks, with the aim of landing them just over the net in the opponent's kitchen. Focus on precision and consistency, trying to maintain a rally where dinks go back and forth without errors. This drill improves your accuracy and helps you develop a feel for how much force to use to keep the ball low and controlled.

Another valuable practice is the dink placement drill. Set up targets within the opponent's non-volley zone—these could be cones, lines, or even specific court tiles. Practice hitting your dinks to these targets from different angles and positions along the net. This drill enhances your ability to control the direction and depth of your dinks, an essential skill during high-pressure game situations where placement can make the difference between winning and losing a point.

You'll notice a significant improvement in your net game by dedicating time to these dinking strategies and drills. The ability to effectively dink enhances your defensive play and sets up offensive opportunities that can lead to winning points. It's a subtle art that, when mastered, provides you with a strategic edge, making you a formidable player who can adeptly control the pace and flow of the game from right up at the net.

2.5 THIRD SHOT DROP: A KEY SKILL FOR ADVANCED PLAYERS

The third shot drop is a crucial skill that can dramatically transform the dynamics of the game from a defensive to an offensive stance. It's a subtle yet powerful shot that occurs typically after the serve and the return, ideally the third shot of the game. This shot is aimed to land softly in the opponent's non-volley zone, also called the kitchen, making it challenging for them to return aggressively. Mastering this technique can greatly increase your ability to control the game and pressure your opponents.

Let's break down the technique for a successful third-shot drop. The key elements to focus on are the paddle angle, your positioning on the court, and the timing of your swing. When executing this shot, your paddle should be angled slightly upwards to ensure the ball arcs gently over the net but drops swiftly into the kitchen. Position your body behind the baseline, allowing yourself enough space to step into the shot and use a forward swing. This position will enable you to leverage gravity and the angle of your paddle to slow down the ball's pace as it crosses the net. Timing is crucial; the ball should be hit just after it reaches its peak height on the bounce, which gives it the necessary trajectory to land softly in the opponent's non-volley zone. A relaxed swing is essential here; too much force will send the ball flying too deep into the court, while a gentle touch will suffice to place it precisely.

The strategic importance of mastering the third shot drop cannot be overstated. This technique allows the serving team to transition from a defensive position at the baseline into an offensive position closer to the net. By successfully dropping the ball into the kitchen, you force your opponents to hit an upward return, which sets you up for a more aggressive follow-up shot, potentially a volley. This puts you in a favorable position to control the rally and make points.

However, several common mistakes can undermine the effectiveness of the third shot drop. One of the most frequent errors is hitting the ball too hard, which usually sends it sailing past the non-volley zone and into the opponent's power zone, where they can hit an aggressive return. To avoid this, focus on a softer touch and practice controlling the swing speed. Another common error is poor placement. If the drop shot is too close to the net, it might not clear it, and if it's too deep, it defeats the purpose of the drop. Practicing precision in your shot placement is critical. Lastly, incorrect body positioning, such as being too close to or too far from the baseline, can affect the angle and trajectory of your shot. Ensure you're in the correct position, giving yourself enough space to execute a controlled and effective drop shot.

Practicing the third shot drop can significantly improve your game. Here are some drills to help you hone this skill. Start with a simple drop shot drill where you repeatedly hit the third shot from the baseline, aiming for the kitchen and focusing on maintaining a soft and controlled swing. You can mark a target area in the kitchen to improve your accuracy. Another effective drill involves moving from the baseline towards the net while executing the third shot drop, which mirrors the actual game scenario where you transition from a defensive to an offensive stance. This drill improves your shot accuracy, court movement, and positioning.

Incorporating these techniques and practice routines into your training will equip you with a robust skill set to handle high-pressure situations in matches. The third shot drop will become a reliable and strategic tool in your pickleball gameplay. With consistent practice, you'll become more confident in turning defensive plays into scoring opportunities, enhancing both your enjoyment and performance in the game.

2.6 DEFENSIVE PLAYS

When it comes to pickleball, having a robust defensive strategy can significantly elevate your game, allowing you to turn potentially tricky situations into opportunities for control and victory. One of the key aspects of a strong defense is the ability to anticipate your opponent's moves. This skill hinges not just on quick reflexes but also on keen observation. By paying close attention to your opponent's positioning and paddle orientation, you can often predict where their next shot will land. For instance, if an opponent's body is angled towards the left corner of your court, there's a good chance their shot will follow that direction. Similarly, the angle of the paddle can give you clues about the height and depth of the upcoming shot. Developing this predictive ability requires practice and a deep understanding of the game's dynamics, which you can enhance by watching skilled players in action or by replaying your matches to observe patterns and outcomes.

Now, let's shift our focus to effectively using court space. Good defensive play isn't just about returning the ball; it's about positioning yourself optimally to make those returns less strenuous and more strategic. Positioning yourself in a way that cuts off angles effectively can limit your opponent's options and force them into making more challenging shots. This might mean staying closer to the center of the baseline to cover both sides of the court equally or moving slightly forward to intercept high shots before they bounce too awkwardly. Efficient movement across the court is also crucial. Instead of running straight to where you think the ball will land, move in a diagonal path, often the shortest route. Also, always try to return to your ready position at the center of the baseline after each shot, as this maximizes your ability to reach the next return, no matter where it lands.

In pickleball, defensive plays often involve various recovery shots, which are crucial when you are out of position or under pressure. Three typical recovery shots are the lob return, the dink, and the reset shot. The lob return is particularly useful when you need to buy some time to get back into position. By sending the ball high and deep into your opponent's court, you force them to move back, thus slowing down the game and giving yourself a chance to recover. On the other hand, the dink is effective when you're close to the net and need to keep the play soft and controlled, aiming to drop the ball just over the net into the non-volley zone. The reset shot is a defensive stroke aimed at neutralizing the pace of the game from a fast volley exchange by returning a soft shot that lands near the net, making it difficult for the opponent to generate offensive power.

Specific drills can be particularly beneficial in building these defensive skills effectively. One helpful exercise is the 'shadow drill' where you move along the baseline, mimicking defensive footwork without actually hitting a ball. This helps improve your lateral movement and agility, which is essential to effective court coverage. Another drill involves practicing recovery shots with a partner or coach who consistently applies pressure by hitting deep and challenging shots. Focus on using lobs, dinks, and resets to regain rally control. This sharpens your shot-making and enhances your ability to stay calm and think strategically under pressure.

Integrating these strategies and drills into your practice sessions will help you develop a defensive game that complements your offensive skills, making you a well-rounded and formidable pickleball player. Remember, a good defense is not just about keeping the ball in play; it's about setting the stage for a strong offense, giving you the upper hand in rallies, and helping you maintain control of the game's pace and flow.

2.7 STRATEGIC POSITIONING AND COURT AWARENESS

Understanding how to move effectively into and out of the non-volley zone can significantly impact your defensive and offensive game. When you're close to the net in the "kitchen," you're in a prime position to react quickly to your opponent's shots and make short, sharp returns that might be harder to achieve from the back of the court. However, the key is not just about stepping into this zone but knowing when to retreat. For instance, if your opponent hits a deep shot, stepping back quickly will give you enough space to handle the shot more efficiently, thus maintaining a strong defensive stance.

Expanding your gameplay to utilize the whole court effectively opens up numerous strategic opportunities. By varying your shots between deep, baseline drives and shorter, angled shots, you can keep your opponent running and guessing, gradually wearing them down or forcing them into a mistake. This strategy involves power, precision and foresight to stretch your opponent's ability to cover the court. For example, after a couple of deep shots that push your opponent back, a well-placed drop shot can catch them off-guard, forcing a sprint toward the net, which may result in a less controlled return.

Anticipating shot returns is another critical skill that can give you a competitive edge. This anticipation starts with keen observation. Pay attention to your opponent's body language, paddle position, and movement. These elements can give you clues about their next shot's likely speed, direction, and style. For instance, a tightly gripped paddle and a forward-leaning stance might indicate a power shot is coming, while a more relaxed grip and upright posture might hint at a softer return. Developing this intuitive sense of prediction requires practice but becomes invaluable in strategic play, allowing you to prepare and position yourself effectively for the next shot.

Positional Drills

Try drills that simulate game-like conditions to enhance your court awareness and strategic positioning. One effective drill is the 'court corners' drill, where you aim to hit each corner of the opponent's court in sequence. This improves your accuracy and helps with your ability to control the ball under varied and strategic conditions. Another beneficial drill involves playing out points where you deliberately only use a specific part of the court, such as only hitting shots that land in the non-volley zone or only using deep baseline shots. This restriction sharpens your skills in those specific areas and improves your overall strategic flexibility.

By mastering strategic positioning and court awareness, you elevate your game from merely reacting to your opponent's shots to actively controlling the flow and pace of the game. This proactive approach enhances your effectiveness on the court. It makes the game more enjoyable as you become adept at outsmarting your opponents and turning potential defensive situations into offensive opportunities.

As we wrap up this chapter on positioning and court awareness, remember that the key to improving in pickleball lies in the continuous application of these strategies. Each game you play is an opportunity to refine your skills, anticipate your opponent's moves, and use the court to your advantage. Keep these techniques in mind as they are fundamental to surviving tough matches and thriving in them, turning challenges into opportunities for victory. Next, we'll dive deeper into enhancing your competitive strategies, ensuring you're well-equipped for whatever comes your way on the court.

ADVANCED STRATEGIES

Whether stepping onto the court for a casual game or gearing up for a competitive match, understanding the subtleties of advanced singles strategy can transform your approach and elevate your game to new heights. Imagine yourself as a chess player, where every move is calculated, and every decision can turn the tide of the game. In singles pickleball, your success hinges not just on your physical prowess but also on your tactical acumen. Let's delve into the strategies to help you outmaneuver your opponents and keep your energy reserves intact for that crucial final point.

3.1 SINGLES STRATEGY

Every player has unique strengths and weaknesses in the dance of singles pickleball, and a big part of your strategy should involve recognizing and exploiting these. For instance, if you notice your opponent hesitates on their backhand, make it your target. Consistently direct your shots to that weaker backhand, and watch as they struggle to return them with the same confidence they might exhibit on their forehand. Similarly, testing their mobility can be effective, especially if they show signs of fatigue or slower movement. Mixing in some well-placed drop shots followed by a lob can force them to move front to back, stretching their stamina and forcing errors.

Conserving your energy during play is crucial, particularly in a sport as dynamic as pickleball. One effective method is to control the pace of the game. This doesn't necessarily mean slowing down the game to a crawl; instead, it's about making deliberate choices about when to ramp up the intensity and when to dial it back. Use strategic shot placement to keep your opponent at the baseline, minimizing your need to engage in a fast-paced volley battle. Additionally, integrate soft dinks into your play. These shots require less physical exertion and can help you catch your breath without completely pausing the action. They also have the added benefit of potentially drawing your opponent into the net, setting you up for a passing shot.

Psychological warfare plays a subtle yet significant role in singles play.

The mental side of pickleball involves:

- Maintaining your focus.
- Managing in-match stress
- Getting into your opponent's head.

Use your body language to your advantage; a confident posture and calm demeanor can mask your fatigue and make you appear unfazed, potentially intimidating your opponent. Varying your shots routinely—alternating between hard drives, soft dinks, and deceptive lobs—can keep your opponent guessing and mentally unsettled, making them more prone to making mistakes.

Preparing for matches is more than just practicing your strokes; it involves studying your upcoming opponents whenever possible. Watch their previous games, noting their preferred shots, weaknesses, and patterns. This knowledge allows you to tailor your strategy to each opponent, effectively adapting your play style to exploit their weaknesses. During the match, stay observant and flexible, ready to tweak your tactics based on the flow of the game and the condition of your opponent. For example, if you see that your opponent is starting to show signs of fatigue, increase the pace and intensity, pushing them to play at a level that might induce more errors.

By embracing these advanced singles strategies, you equip yourself with a toolkit designed to play the game smartly. This approach ensures you're always two steps ahead, turning each match into a test of skill and a display of strategic mastery.

3.2 DOUBLES PLAY: COORDINATION AND COMMUNICATION

In doubles pickleball, the harmony between partners is just as crucial as individual skill. Imagine a well-coordinated dance where each step and each move is in perfect harmony. That's what effective doubles play should feel like. It involves a dynamic exchange of non-verbal cues and brief verbal commands that can dramatically streamline your gameplay. Non-verbal signals, such as paddle signals or specific positioning, can silently inform your partner of your next move, allowing seamless play without giving away your strategy to opponents. Verbal cues, such as "yours," "mine," or "leave," help make split-second decisions together. This method of communication prevents overlaps where both players go for the ball at the same time.

Now, let's talk about the roles each player assumes in doubles. Typically, one player adopts a more aggressive role, often staying at the baseline to drive powerful shots. In contrast, the other adopts a more defensive role, focusing on net play and precision. These roles are not fixed and can shift dynamically throughout the match, depending on the situation and the opponent's strategy. For instance, if the defensive player sees an opportunity to make an aggressive shot, they should momentarily switch roles. This fluidity can keep opponents off-balance and open the court for more strategic plays. However, this requires a deep understanding of each other's strengths, weaknesses, and tendencies, which is why regular practice and communication are crucial.

Covering the court effectively in doubles play involves strategic positioning and constant adjustments. Common formations include both players at the net, which is aggressive and ideal for volley exchanges; one player at the net and one player back, providing balance and coverage; and both players back, which is defensive and helpful against strong opponents. Each formation has its strengths and vulnerabilities, and a key part of your strategy is knowing when to switch formations. For example, if you and your partner are at the net and the opponents lob the ball over your heads, the player closest to the ball's trajectory should turn and retrieve it while the other moves to cover the middle of the court. This switch should be fluid, quick, and communicated through a quick shout or hand signal to avoid confusion.

Practicing as a team is essential to refine these movements and strategies. Drills that enhance team coordination are invaluable. Start with side-by-side movements where both players move laterally across the court in sync, maintaining a position that allows quick volleys and minimizes gaps. This drill not only improves your ability to move as a unit but also helps develop a sense of how much court each player can cover. Another effective drill is the front-back movement drill. One player starts at the net while the other starts at the baseline, and the goal is to switch positions fluidly on each shot, mimicking the quick role reversals that might happen in a game. Lastly, synchronized volleying practice, where both players volley back and forth with a third player or coach, can sharpen your reflexes and improve your net game.

These exercises build the intuition and trust necessary for effective doubles play. They help you and your partner understand each other's playing style deeply, predict each other's moves, and operate as a single unit, adapting fluidly to whatever the game throws at you. As you continue to practice and communicate, your coordination improves, making your doubles game not just a display of individual skills but a showcase of seamless partnership and strategic finesse.

3.3 VARIANTS: SKINNY SINGLES AND MORE

Pickleball, as you've probably discovered, is wonderfully adaptable, offering various formats that cater to different skills, spaces, and numbers of players. While traditional singles and doubles are the most recognized forms, variations like Skinny Singles bring a fresh twist to the game, focusing play on a narrower section of the court. In Skinny Singles, you use only one half of the court, which intensifies the game by limiting the area each player must cover. This variant sharpens your aim and enhances your ability to control the ball with precision.

Playing Skinny Singles requires you to adapt the standard rules slightly. The court is divided lengthwise, and each player is responsible for only one side, like playing singles on a half-court. This setup increases the game's difficulty as it demands greater accuracy and control. The narrower playing area means less ground to cover, which might seem easier at first glance, but it increases the need for precise shot placement and quick reflexes. Players find that this variant enhances their ability to focus and fine-tune their motor skills, as any slight misjudgment can send the ball into the out-of-bounds area.

The benefits of playing variants like Skinny Singles or traditional singles are substantial. For instance, in conventional singles, the wider court demands excellent stamina and the ability to cover more ground, which can help improve your overall fitness levels. The extended reach required can also enhance your agility and cardiovascular health. On the other hand, Skinny Singles can be particularly beneficial in honing your precision and strategic thinking. It forces you to make every shot count and to think several moves ahead, anticipating your opponent's returns with much greater accuracy.

These game variations can be especially enjoyable and beneficial in different scenarios. For example, if you have limited space, such as a smaller backyard or a shared gym space, playing Skinny Singles can allow you to enjoy the game without needing a full-sized court. It's also ideal if you have an odd number of players; while some engage in a doubles match, others can play Skinny Singles, ensuring everyone stays active and involved.

Organizing tournaments or social gatherings that feature these variants can significantly enrich your pickleball community's experience. To set up a variant tournament, clearly define the rules and court modifications needed so all participants are on the same page. It's also a good idea to have some practice sessions before the tournament to help players adjust to the differences in play style required by these formats. Promote these events as opportunities to learn new skills, meet other players, and break the routine of standard play. This brings excitement to your pickleball sessions and fosters a spirit of innovation and adaptability within your community.

Integrating these varied forms of pickleball into your playing routine opens up a new layer of challenge and engagement, pushing yourself and your fellow players to refine different aspects of your game. Whether improving your stamina on the full court or enhancing your precision in Skinny Singles, these variants ensure your pickleball experience remains fresh, enjoyable, and continually evolving.

PHYSICAL AND MENTAL FITNESS

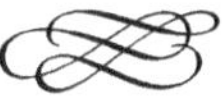

Think of pickleball not just as a sport but as a dance that engages every muscle in your body, demanding strength and grace and a sharp mind that keeps pace with the quick volleys. This chapter is your gym session, where we sculpt the body and mind to play and excel at pickleball. It's about conditioning yourself so that when you step onto that court, your body moves as if it's on autopilot, powerful and precise, and your mind, clear and focused, ready for whatever the game throws at you.

4.1 PICKLEBALL-SPECIFIC FITNESS

Tailored Strength Training

When you're on the court, every serve, volley, and sprint relies on the symphony of muscles working in harmony. Let's zoom in on a few exercises that target those key muscle groups most engaged during a pickleball game. For instance, your quadriceps and hamstrings are pivotal for those quick sprints and sudden stops. Squats and lunges are your best friends here. They mimic the lower-body movements you make during a game; strengthening these muscles will increase your speed and stability on the court.

Then there are your shoulders, essential for every serve and smash. Shoulder presses and lateral raises will build strength in these areas and enhance your endurance, allowing you to play those long, intense rallies without faltering.

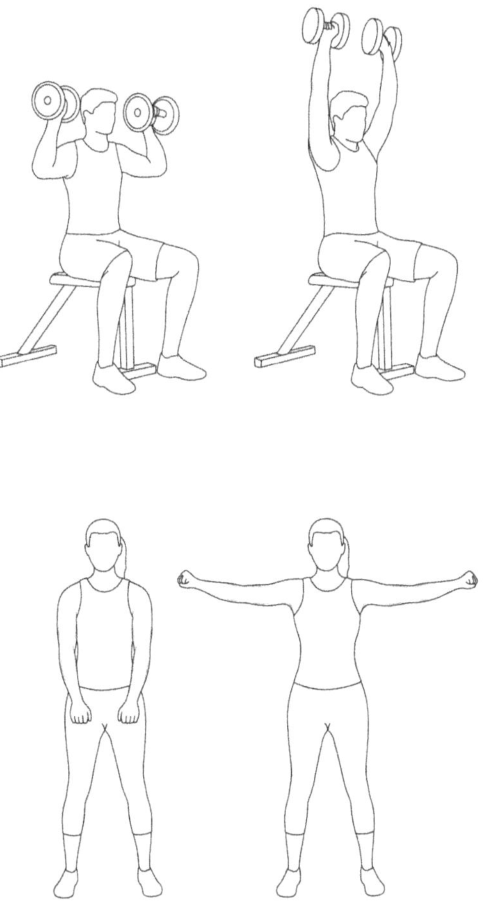

Each of these exercises boosts your performance and shields you against injuries, ensuring that each muscle is prepped to handle the specific demands of pickleball. Integrating these exercises into your routine about two to three times a week can significantly improve your game, making you a stronger, more resilient player.

Cardiovascular Endurance

Next up, let's get your heart rate up. Pickleball requires bursts of speed and quick recovery, making cardiovascular fitness non-negotiable. Interval training is perfect for this; it mirrors the stop-and-start nature of a typical pickleball game. Picture this: you sprint to the baseline to return a deep shot, pause to anticipate your opponent's next move, and then dash toward the net for a volley. Training your body to handle these bursts of activity, followed by periods of lighter recovery (walking or slow jogging), will enhance your stamina and recovery speed.

Here is an example:

Sample Interval Run Training Exercise (20 Minutes):

Warm-Up (3 minutes):

- Start with 2 minutes of light jogging to get your heart rate up.
- Spend 1 minute doing dynamic stretches like high knees and leg swings to loosen up your muscles.

Interval Run Workout (14 minutes):

1. Interval 1: Sprint

- Duration: 30 seconds
- Run at 85-90% of your maximum effort, focusing on speed and form.

2. Interval 2: Recovery Jog

- Duration: 1 minute
- Jog at a comfortable pace to bring your heart rate down slightly.

3. Interval 3: Uphill Run

- Duration: 30 seconds
- Find an incline or hill and run up at a challenging pace, driving your knees and maintaining good posture.

4. Interval 4: Walk

- Duration: 1 minute
- Walk at a moderate pace to recover, keeping your legs moving.

5. Interval 5: Fartlek Run

- Duration: 2 minutes
- Alternate between 20 seconds of sprinting and 40 seconds of jogging. This will vary your intensity within a single interval.

6. Interval 6: Recovery Walk

- Duration: 1 minute
- Walk at a relaxed pace to allow your heart rate to lower.

7. Interval 7: Tempo Run

- Duration: 3 minutes
- Run at a steady, challenging pace, slightly faster than your usual running speed. Maintain this pace throughout.

8. Interval 8: Cool Down

- Duration: 2.5 minutes
- Gradually slow down to a light jog and then to a brisk walk. Finish with one minute of static stretches, focusing on your calves, hamstrings, and quadriceps.

Total Duration: 20 minutes

Notes:

- Adjust the intensity of the intervals based on your fitness level.
- For beginners, slightly reduce sprint and uphill intervals and increase recovery time.
- As you get fitter, aim to increase the intensity of the sprint and tempo intervals.

Goal: This quick, high-intensity interval session is designed to improve your cardiovascular fitness and running speed in just 20 minutes.

Agility and Flexibility Workouts

Now, let's make sure you can reach that seemingly impossible shot. Agility drills such as ladder or cone drills enhance your ability to change direction quickly—an indispensable skill on the pickleball court. These drills improve your footwork, making your movements more efficient and less energy-consuming. Pairing agility with flexibility exercises, like dynamic stretching before games and static stretching afterward, ensures that your muscles are limber and more responsive during gameplay. This routine improves your range of motion and reduces the risk of injuries by ensuring your muscles and joints are well-conditioned for the quick pivots and stretches that are so common in a match.

Recovery Practices

Finally, let's talk about what you do after stepping off the court, which is just as important as the game itself. Proper cooldown routines help transition your body back to its normal state, reducing the likelihood of post-exercise soreness. Gentle stretching, hydration, and nutrition play critical roles here. Make sure you drink plenty of fluids to replace what you've lost through sweat and eat a balanced meal with proteins to rebuild muscles and carbohydrates to replenish energy stores. Don't underestimate the power of a good night's sleep, which is when most muscle repair occurs. Ensuring you get enough rest helps in physical recovery and prepares your mind for the mental challenges of the next game.

By incorporating these fitness and recovery strategies into your routine, you're preparing your body for the physical demands of pickleball and setting a foundation for continuous improvement and enjoyment in the sport. Whether playing a casual game with friends or competing in a tournament, your body and mind will be primed for peak performance, ready to handle whatever the game might bring.

4.2 MENTAL TOUGHNESS FOR COMPETITIVE PLAY

Stepping onto the pickleball court for a competitive match is as much a mental challenge as a physical one. Have you ever noticed how some players seem unshakeable, turning the tide of the game even under high pressure? Much of this resilience starts long before the match begins, with robust pre-game routines. Establishing a pre-game routine is similar to setting the stage for a great performance; it primes your mind to enter a state of focused readiness. Consider incorporating mental warm-ups into your routine, just as you would physical stretches. Visualization can be a powerful tool here. Spend a few minutes visualizing successful plays, imagining the feel of the paddle, the sound of the ball hitting the sweet spot, and even the victorious moments of scoring points. This mental rehearsal boosts your confidence and calms nerves, effectively setting a positive tone for gameplay.

Another component of your mental toolkit should be techniques that enhance your focus and concentration during the game. Distractions are inevitable, whether from a noisy crowd or the internal pressure of a tight scoreline. Practices like mindfulness meditation can significantly enhance your ability to remain present and focused. Even simple breathing techniques, such as deep, controlled breaths, can help maintain calm and focus during those critical game moments. These exercises train your mind to stay centered and clear, preventing external and internal disruptions from affecting your performance. Engaging in short mindfulness sessions daily, even for just five to ten minutes, can train your brain to maintain this focused state naturally during games.

Building and maintaining self-confidence is another cornerstone of mental toughness in competitive play. Confidence on the court doesn't just sprout overnight; it's cultivated through consistent practice and mental conditioning. Techniques like visualization, which prepares you for the game and reinforces a self-image of success and competence, play a crucial role here. Another effective strategy is success journaling. After each game or practice session, take a few minutes to jot down what went well. This could be a particularly good shot, a strategy that paid off, or your ability to stay calm under pressure. This habit reinforces positive self-perception and builds a reservoir of successful experiences that you can draw confidence from in future matches.

Handling losses and setbacks with grace and resilience is one of the most challenging aspects of competitive sports. No one likes to lose, but setbacks are inevitable and are rich with lessons. The key is to approach them constructively. After a loss, analyze the game instead of dwelling on disappointment to understand what didn't work and why. This constructive self-assessment can help you identify areas for improvement, whether it's a skill that needs sharpening or a strategic error that needs rethinking. Additionally, engaging in resilience-building practices such as reflecting on past comeback stories, personal or from athletes you admire, can motivate you to bounce back stronger. Remember, resilience isn't about not falling; it's about learning how to get back up, equipped with better strategies and a stronger mindset.

By weaving these mental fitness strategies into your routine, you equip yourself with a robust mental framework that complements your physical skills, ensuring you're not just playing the game but are mentally sculpted to excel in it. Mental toughness can be your ultimate ally on the competitive pickleball court, whether it's through enhancing your pre-game preparation, sharpening your focus, building unwavering confidence, or mastering the art of comeback.

4.3 HOW TO STAY FOCUSED UNDER PRESSURE

The clamor of the crowd, the score ticking closer to the game point, and the weight of expectation can all amplify the pressure you feel during a pickleball match. Understanding how this pressure impacts you can be the difference between a win and a loss. When under stress, your body releases hormones like adrenaline and cortisol, heightening your senses and quickening your pulse. The release of these hormones can enhance your performance by sharpening your focus and reactions. However, they can also overwhelm you, leading to hasty decisions or physical tension that detracts from your game. Your brain might focus more on potential negative outcomes, like missing a shot or losing the match, which can cloud your decision-making and reduce your effectiveness on the court.

Managing this stress effectively is crucial, and several strategies can help. Controlled breathing techniques are a powerful tool. Focusing on deep, steady breaths can counteract your body's stress response, maintaining both physical and mental calm. Think of it as hitting a reset button, helping to clear your mind and steady your nerves. Another helpful technique is focusing on one point at a time. Pickleball, like life, is best tackled one step at a time. Concentrate solely on the point at hand, not the previous ones or those yet to come. This approach keeps you present and can significantly reduce the pressure of the moment. Positive self-talk also plays a critical role in managing stress. Encourage yourself with affirmations or remind yourself of past successes when you feel pressure mounting. This kind of mental cheering section can boost your morale and refocus your mind on positive outcomes rather than dwelling on potential mistakes.

Emotional control during matches is another vital skill that can set you apart from competitors. Staying composed after a bad shot or a challenging point can keep your head in the game and your strategy sharp. Everyone makes mistakes, but keeping them from defining your game is key. Take a moment, if needed, to regroup. A quick walk to the back of the court or a moment spent adjusting your grip can be a physical reset and a mental break, allowing you to let go of the error and refocus on the next point. Moreover, learning to channel your emotions into positive energy rather than frustration or anger can transform potentially disruptive feelings into motivation to improve and push harder.

Supporting your mental health outside the court is just as important as any physical training. Regular practices like yoga can enhance both your physical flexibility and mental resilience. Focusing on mindful movement and breathwork in yoga can improve stress management, translating well into high-pressure game situations. Maintaining a balanced lifestyle, which includes adequate sleep, a nutritious diet, and regular physical activity, also supports your mental and emotional well-being, keeping you sharp and focused both on and off the court. Furthermore, don't hesitate to seek professional guidance if you find stress and pressure affect your enjoyment of the game or your performance more broadly. Sometimes, a few sessions with a sports psychologist or a mental performance coach can provide you with strategies and perspectives that make all the difference.

As we wrap up this exploration of physical and mental fitness, remember that pickleball is more than just a game of skill and strategy; it's a dance of mental agility and physical prowess, where each point challenges your body and your mind. By nurturing both, you prepare to meet every serve, volley, and dink confidently, no matter the pressure. Keep these tips in mind as you continue to refine your skills and strategies, and look forward to the next chapter, where we delve into the nuances of drills and practice that can further enhance your performance and enjoyment of pickleball.

DRILLS AND PRACTICE

I magine stepping onto the pickleball court, your paddle in hand, feeling that rush of confidence because you know you've done the work off the court to sharpen your skills. Drills and practice might not be as thrilling as a match but think of them as your secret weapon. The more you train, the more your movements and strategies become more natural during gameplay. This chapter is dedicated to transforming how you practice, making each session as productive as possible so that it all feels like second nature when you play.

5.1 SOLO DRILLS

Target Practice for Accuracy

Nothing beats good old target practice when it comes to improving your shot precision. It's like playing darts but with your pickleball paddle. Start by placing targets at strategic locations across the court. These could be anything from a brightly colored towel, cones, or even specific court tiles. The key here is to create a scenario that mimics real game situations. Try placing a target in each corner of the service box to ensure your service accuracy. The goal is to hit each target with your serve, adjusting your angle and power with each attempt. This sharpens your serving skills and enhances your ability to start the game on a strong note.

Dink placement is another critical skill; setting up a target in the non-volley zone can drastically improve your proficiency. Practice hitting your dinks softly, aiming for precision rather than power. The softer your shot, the more challenging it is for your opponent to return it with strength. This drill improves your accuracy and teaches you control and finesse, turning the dink into a powerful tool in your game arsenal.

Ladder Drills for Speed and Agility

Speed and agility are your best allies on the pickleball court. Ladder drills are a fantastic way to enhance these attributes. Set up an agility ladder on the ground near your playing area. The sequence involves a variety of footwork patterns—such as the two-foot run, in-and-out hop, or lateral shuffles. Each pattern challenges different muscle groups and coordination skills, which are crucial for those quick, explosive movements needed during a game. As you move through the ladder, focus on maintaining a quick, light touch of the feet and a steady pace. This drill boosts your footwork and increases your overall agility, making it easier to reach those tough shots.

Wall Rallies for Consistency and Reaction Time

Practicing against a wall can significantly enhance paddle control and develop consistent stroke mechanics. Find a solid wall, like at a racquetball court or even a handball wall at your local park, and start with simple forehand and backhand strokes. The goal is to hit the ball against the wall and allow it to bounce once before returning it. This drill mirrors the rhythm and pace of an actual game and improves your reaction time significantly. Try to keep the rally going as long as possible, increasing your speed and reducing the time between hits as you improve. This enhances stroke consistency and trains you to respond more quickly under pressure.

Endurance Drills for Longer Play

Pickleball games can sometimes stretch longer than anticipated, and maintaining a high energy level becomes crucial. Endurance drills can be a game-changer here. Set up a drill that mimics the stop-and-go nature of pickleball. You could use the entire length of the court, starting at one baseline, sprinting to the net to simulate a volley, and jogging back. Repeat this sequence several times, gradually increasing the intensity and duration. This builds your stamina and mimics the actual game's physical demands, preparing you to maintain your performance level throughout extended play periods.

By incorporating these solo drills into your routine, you're not just practicing; you're sculpting your skills, refining your techniques, and boosting your confidence, one shot at a time. Each session on the court or against the wall is an investment in your game, turning potential weaknesses into strengths and making you a formidable player who's ready for anything the match brings.

5.2 PARTNER DRILLS

The game takes on a new dimension when you step onto the pickleball court with a partner. It's no longer just about your skills or reactions; it's about how well you move as a unit, anticipate each other's actions, and communicate silently yet effectively. That's where partner drills come into play, transforming two individual players into a synchronized team ready to dominate the court.

Mirror Drills for Synchronized Movement

Mirror drills are one of the most dynamic ways to achieve this synchronization. Here, you and your partner mimic each other's movements across the court, mirroring each other's steps, swings, and stances. Start on opposite sides of the net and move in sync—when one steps forward, the other does too; when one swings, the other mirrors the action. This drill enhances your spatial awareness and understanding of court positioning. It teaches you to stay in tune with your partner's movements, which is crucial during actual gameplay, where anticipating each other's position and reach can make the difference between a point won and a point lost. As you progress, increase the complexity of the movements and include more game-like scenarios, such as mimicking a series of volleys and groundstrokes, enhancing your physical coordination and strategic alignment.

Rotational Drills for Fluid Positioning

In doubles play, fluidity in switching positions with your partner—rotating between offensive and defensive roles—is vital to maintaining pressure on your opponents and covering the court effectively. Rotational drills are designed to perfect this dance. Set up a drill where you and your partner continuously switch from front to back positions in response to your shot selections. For example, if you move up to the net to take a volley, your partner should simultaneously move back to cover the baseline, and vice versa. This rotation needs to be smooth and seamless, with each player aware of the space they need to cover. Practice this drill with a variety of shots and from different angles to simulate game situations. This improves your physical agility and sharpens your tactical understanding of when and how to switch roles during a match.

Communication Drills for Non-verbal Signals

Effective communication on the court often relies on non-verbal cues, which can be as simple as a nod, a pointed paddle, or a specific positioning of your body. These signals are crucial for silent strategizing and ensuring you and your partner are always on the same page. Practice drills where you develop and use your own set of non-verbal signals to indicate various play strategies. For instance, holding the paddle up could mean you're taking the next shot, while a paddle pointed toward the ground could mean you're setting up a defensive play. Work these signals into regular play drills to make them automatic. This silent language between you can be incredibly powerful, especially in high-pressure situations where spoken words might not be heard.

Cooperative Rally Drills to Build Rhythm

Building a rhythmic flow with your partner is crucial for maintaining momentum in a game. Engage in cooperative rally drills where the goal is to maintain a volley for a set number of exchanges or to target different zones of the court consecutively. Start with slow, controlled rallies, focusing on consistency and placement. Gradually increase the pace and intensity, challenging each other to maintain the rhythm under demanding conditions. These drills improve your technical skills and enhance your ability to read the game and your partner's play style, adjusting your responses in real-time to maintain the flow and pressure.

Through these partner drills, you're not just practicing skills but building a partnership that understands, anticipates, moves, and reacts as one unit. This unity can be your greatest strength in doubles play, turning individual efforts into a collective performance that is both fluid and formidable. Embrace these drills to deepen your connection with your partner and refine your strategies, making every match you play a testament to the power of teamwork.

5.3 GAME SCENARIO DRILLS

Imagine yourself in the heat of a close pickleball match where every point feels like it could tip the scales. The pressure is palpable. This is where our first type of drill, designed to simulate match conditions, comes into play. Picture setting up a game where you're down by a few points, and you have to fight your way back under a time constraint. This not only mimics the pressure cooker environment of a competitive match but also teaches you to keep your cool and strategize under stress. You could set a timer and start each game with a score deficit, say 5-8, challenging yourself to overcome the lead before time runs out. These drills push you to make smart, swift decisions, enhancing your ability to perform when the pressure mounts in actual games.

Switching gears, let's talk about tactical drills that require quick thinking and adaptability. Imagine a drill where your coach or a partner calls out random shots during a rally, demanding immediate adjustment and execution. One moment, you're asked to hit a deep baseline shot; the next, a soft dink into the kitchen. This keeps you on your toes, ready to switch your game plan at a moment's notice. Such exercises are invaluable because, during actual matches, conditions change rapidly, and your ability to adapt can be the difference between winning and losing a point. These drills train your mind and body to handle sudden shifts in play style, making you a more versatile and unpredictable player.

Now, let's delve into role-playing critical game moments. This type of drill involves creating scenarios that replicate crucial points in a match, like a tiebreaker or a game-winning shot. It's about more than just playing; it's about embodying the moment. Set up a scenario where the score is tied at 10-10, and every point feels like a mountain to climb. Practicing these high-stakes situations prepares you not just physically but emotionally, helping you manage the nerves and tension that come with such moments. The focus here is on maintaining precision in your shots and steadiness in your decisions, ensuring that when real opportunities arise in matches, you're ready to seize them with confidence.

Lastly, the value of reviewing and analyzing your performance post-drill cannot be overstated. Whether it's a video recording of your practice or a coach's feedback, reviewing your drills can open your eyes to habits you might not realize you have or strategies that could be tweaked for better results. This reflective practice helps reinforce what works and correct what doesn't, turning each drill session into a stepping stone toward becoming a more skilled player.

Through these game scenario drills, you refine your technical skills and enhance your mental and emotional readiness, mirroring the challenges you'll face in actual competitive play. Each drill is a building block, fortifying your game from the ground up, ensuring that when the pressure is on, you're not just ready; you're in control.

As we wrap up this chapter on drills and practice, remember that the ultimate goal of these exercises is to bridge the gap between practice and play. It's about transforming your hard work into tangible improvements on the court, where strategic decisions, swift adaptations, and steady nerves come together to elevate your game.

ADAPTIVE PICKLEBALL

Imagine stepping onto a pickleball court where every detail, from the paddle in your hand to the shoes on your feet, is tailored to your unique needs and abilities. This chapter is dedicated to transforming the game of pickleball into an inclusive sport that welcomes players of all abilities, ensuring that everyone, regardless of physical limitations, can experience the joy and excitement of the game. Here, we delve into the world of adaptive pickleball, focusing on how equipment and technology can be customized to enhance accessibility and enjoyment for every player.

6.1 EQUIPMENT MODIFICATIONS

Customizing Paddles for Better Grip

For many players, the paddle is the most crucial piece of equipment. However, standard paddles may only sometimes accommodate everyone's needs, especially for players with limited hand function. Customizing or choosing a paddle with a modified grip can make a significant difference. Larger, foam-padded grips can provide better control and reduce strain for those who might have difficulty grasping a standard handle. Ergonomically shaped grips, which are designed to fit more naturally in the hand, can also help reduce the effort needed to hold and swing the paddle effectively. These modifications enhance comfort and improve the player's ability to play longer and with more confidence. Imagine a paddle that feels like an extension of your hand, where every serve and volley is executed with ease and precision—this is the goal of customized grip adaptations.

Wheelchair-Friendly Equipment

Adapting equipment for wheelchair users is another crucial aspect of making pickleball accessible. Wheelchairs designed specifically for pickleball are lighter and more maneuverable, allowing quicker turns and better stability on the court. These chairs often feature enhanced wheel-locking mechanisms to ensure safety during play, and their design minimizes the risk of tipping, providing players with the confidence to reach and move freely. Additionally, paddles with lighter materials reduce the physical strain for players who need to balance paddle control with wheelchair maneuvers. These adaptations ensure wheelchair players can compete successfully and fully enjoy the game, focusing on their strategy and skill rather than being hindered by unsuitable equipment.

Adaptive Clothing and Accessories

Comfort on the court extends beyond just paddles and wheelchairs. Adaptive clothing and accessories are vital in ensuring that all players can move freely and comfortably. Clothing made from non-restrictive, breathable fabrics allows for better airflow, keeping players cool during intense matches. Shoes with enhanced grip designs provide additional safety and performance on various court surfaces, crucial for players who need extra stability and support. These clothing options not only cater to functional needs but also ensure that players feel confident and at ease, allowing them to focus solely on their game and enjoyment.

Use of Assistive Technology

Recent advancements in assistive technology have created new opportunities for adaptive pickleball. For instance, paddles equipped with built-in sensors can provide real-time feedback on swing technique, helping players refine their strokes and improve their game. For visually impaired players, balls equipped with audible signals that beep or ring help in tracking the ball during play. This technology enables players who would otherwise find it challenging to follow the fast-paced game to participate fully and competitively. It's a beautiful blend of technology and sport, where innovative solutions bring the joy of pickleball to a broader audience, ensuring no one is left on the sidelines.

By embracing these modifications and technologies, pickleball becomes a sport where limitations are transformed into opportunities for innovation and enjoyment. Each adaptation not only enhances accessibility but also enriches the playing experience, ensuring that pickleball remains a beloved and inclusive sport for generations to come.

6.2 ADAPTIVE STRATEGIES

When it comes to playing pickleball, the joy and challenge of the game should be accessible to everyone, regardless of physical ability. For wheelchair users, mastering the game involves strategic positioning and movement patterns that can significantly enhance their play. Wheelchair players can quickly pivot and maneuver from a seated position, which can be particularly useful near the net. To optimize these movements, positioning yourself slightly behind the baseline can provide a broader range of reach and more time to react to volleys. It's also beneficial to practice rolling forward to reach shots rather than relying solely on arm reach, as this can increase your range and power. Additionally, practicing quick stops and starts can enhance your ability to control the wheelchair on the court, making it easier to adjust your position as the game progresses.

Adapting the rules of pickleball to accommodate players with disabilities can also make the game more inclusive and enjoyable. One common modification is allowing the ball to bounce twice instead of once before returning it. This adjustment can provide players who require more time for movement, such as those in wheelchairs or with mobility impairments, the opportunity to position themselves effectively to make a shot. Another possible modification is adjusting the size of the non-volley zone or kitchen. By slightly increasing this area, players who find rapid forward movement challenging can still actively participate in volleys and soft gameplay at the net, ensuring they remain integral competitors in the game.

For players with visual impairments, pickleball can be adapted in ways that allow the sense of hearing to take precedence. Using balls that emit sounds such as beeping or ringing can help visually impaired players locate the ball during play. These auditory cues enable players to react to the ball's position and trajectory, making the game more accessible. Developing strong verbal communication skills with partners and opponents can significantly enhance gameplay. Clear, concise announcements of shots, such as "yours" or "mine," and updates on the score or ball position help maintain an inclusive game environment. Practicing these communication skills can foster teamwork and ensure all players are engaged and informed throughout the game.

Building team dynamics in pickleball, especially among players of mixed abilities, is crucial for fostering a supportive and competitive environment. Understanding and adapting to each player's strengths and limitations can create a team where everyone contributes meaningfully. For instance, a player with strong strategic thinking but limited mobility might focus on shot placement and tactics. In contrast, a more mobile player might take on roles that require quick movements and extensive court coverage. Regular practice sessions where players openly discuss their capabilities and strategies can help form a cohesive unit that values each member's contributions. Additionally, implementing drills that focus on adaptive techniques can ensure that all team members are equipped with the skills and confidence to play effectively, regardless of their physical abilities.

By embracing these adaptive strategies, pickleball becomes a sport that truly exemplifies inclusivity and competition. Every player, regardless of physical challenges, can find enjoyment, improvement, and camaraderie. Through thoughtful adaptations and a commitment to understanding individual needs, players and coaches can transform standard games into extraordinary opportunities for all to excel and participate fully.

6.3 ORGANIZE INCLUSIVE SESSIONS

Creating an environment that welcomes players of all abilities starts with the very infrastructure of your pickleball facilities. When designing or adapting spaces for pickleball, ensuring accessibility involves considering various elements that cater to a diverse range of needs. For instance, wheelchair-friendly court surfaces are not only about smoothness but also about the firmness that prevents wheels from sinking or catching, which can disrupt play and pose safety risks. These surfaces should provide enough traction for secure movement while being gentle enough to minimize wear and tear on wheelchair tires. Additionally, adequate lighting is crucial, especially for players with low vision. It should be bright enough to illuminate the entire court evenly without creating glare or shadows that make it difficult to see the ball. Moreover, clearly marked boundaries using high-contrast colors can significantly aid players in quickly and accurately assessing their position relative to the court's limits, enhancing both the safety and enjoyment of the game.

When it comes to programming, inclusivity means more than just allowing everyone to play—it means actively facilitating a range of abilities to engage fully with the sport. Structuring pickleball programs requires thoughtful scheduling that allocates dedicated times for players of different skill levels and physical capabilities. This can involve sessions specifically designed for wheelchair users, those who are visually impaired, and even family-friendly sessions where adaptations are made to ensure everyone, from the youngest to the oldest, can participate safely. In addition, providing adaptive training—coaching that recognizes and addresses the unique needs of each participant—ensures that all players not only participate but also improve and thrive. Offering competitive opportunities is equally important, as competition can be a significant motivator. Organizing tournaments and leagues that categorize players based on ability rather than just age or gender can lead to more meaningful and enjoyable competition.

Educational workshops and clinics are pivotal platforms for spreading knowledge about adaptive pickleball techniques and the importance of inclusivity in sports. These sessions can educate players, coaches, and facility managers on the nuances of adaptive sports equipment, the benefits of inclusive sports programs, and effective strategies for enhancing accessibility. Such education raises awareness and empowers individuals to become advocates for inclusivity within their communities, promoting a broader cultural shift towards more accessible sports practices.

Promoting social inclusion goes beyond physical and programmatic adaptations; it fosters a community spirit that values and celebrates diversity. Organizing social mixers, team-building activities, and family-friendly events are fantastic ways to encourage interactions among players of all abilities, creating a welcoming and supportive community. These events can include mixed-ability games, where teams are composed of players with varying ability levels, encouraging cooperation and learning from each other. Social mixers can also feature fun, non-competitive games focusing on enjoyment and interaction rather than scores and performance. By regularly bringing people together in a setting that values fun and camaraderie over winning, you reinforce the idea that pickleball is more than just a game—it's a community activity that enriches lives.

Organizing inclusive sessions in pickleball is about creating environments and experiences that recognize and respect individual differences while promoting a sense of community and enjoyment for all. It's about ensuring that every element, from the facility design to the programming and community engagement activities, contributes to an atmosphere where everyone feels valued, included, and eager to return. As we move forward into the next chapter, we'll explore how the principles of inclusion can be applied in recreational settings and competitive arenas, ensuring that pickleball remains a sport beloved by all, regardless of ability.

PICKLEBALL FOR ALL AGES

7.1 CHILDREN

Imagine stepping onto a pickleball court, buzzing with children's vibrant energy, all eager to smack a lightweight ball over the net with paddles just the right size for their little hands. Introducing children to pickleball isn't just about teaching them a new sport—it's about opening the door to a world of active play, teamwork, and fun. Let's dive into how we can simplify the rules, design engaging games, choose the right equipment, and cultivate sportsmanship, making this sport a favorite for the younger crowd.

Simplified Rules for Quick Learning

When it comes to young players, simplicity is key. The rules of pickleball, while straightforward, can be tweaked to ensure that children grasp them easily and quickly. For starters, consider simplifying the scoring system. Instead of the standard 11-point game with a 2-point lead requirement, you might introduce games that are played to just 5 or 7 points. This not only keeps the game duration ideal for shorter attention spans but also brings the thrill of a quick win closer, keeping them excited and engaged.

Furthermore, the non-volley zone, or "the kitchen," rule can be a bit complex for kids to remember. In the beginning, allowing them to volley from anywhere might be helpful, removing this restriction until they get more comfortable with their paddle skills and movement around the court. As they advance, gradually introduce the concept of the kitchen and its rules, turning it into a learning game where they're rewarded for remembering to bounce the ball in this zone.

Games for Skill Development

Children thrive in playful learning environments, and pickleball is ideally suited for games that are both fun and educational. Create mini-games that focus on specific skills. For example, "Pickle Pirates," a game where children have to "steal" balls from the other side of the court and bring them back to their ship (side of the court), can be a thrilling way to teach them about court boundaries and movement. Another game, "Paddle Balloon," where kids keep a balloon in the air using their paddles, can help improve hand-eye coordination and paddle handling in a fun, stress-free way.

These games keep the children engaged and allow them to develop essential pickleball skills like serving, volleying, and scoring in a context that feels more like play and less like training. It's about making the learning process enjoyable and memorable, ensuring they return to the court enthusiastically.

Equipment Suitable for Children

The right equipment can make all the difference in ensuring safety and enhancing the play experience for children. Lightweight paddles are a must; they're easier for small hands to handle and lessen the risk of strain or injury. Many brands offer junior paddles that are perfect for younger players. They are made from lightweight materials and feature smaller grips.

Similarly, opting for softer, lighter balls can make the game safer and more enjoyable for kids.

These balls are easier to hit and less intimidating, making the learning process more encouraging. Always check that the equipment meets safety standards and is appropriate for the age group you are coaching or playing with, ensuring a safe playing environment for everyone.

Encouraging Sportsmanship and Team Play

Pickleball offers a fantastic platform to instill values like sportsmanship and teamwork from an early age. Teach children to respect their opponents and teammates, encouraging handshakes or paddle taps after games, regardless of the outcome. Emphasize the importance of fair play and taking turns, and use team drills to foster collaboration. For instance, setting up doubles games where kids need to communicate and work together to score can effectively teach them about teamwork in real-game scenarios.

Additionally, integrate discussions about the rules and ethics of the game into your sessions. This not only helps children understand why these rules exist but also helps them appreciate the value of playing by the rules, which is a critical aspect of sportsmanship.

By focusing on these foundational elements, you create a pickleball experience for children that is about learning a new sport and growing in skill and character. It's about giving them tools beyond the court, helping them develop into team players and respectful competitors. Whether they pursue pickleball seriously or just play for fun, these early lessons will enrich their sports experience and teach them values that last a lifetime.

7.2 SENIORS

Pickleball has a unique charm for seniors. It offers a blend of gentle physical exercise and lively social interaction that can significantly enhance quality of life. Regular pickleball play can improve mobility, helping to maintain or even improve range of motion and flexibility. These physical activities are crucial for managing or preventing age-related conditions such as arthritis and osteoporosis. Moreover, the game's cardiovascular aspect helps maintain heart health and regulate blood pressure, which are vital components of senior health.

Beyond the physical, pickleball offers just as valuable cognitive benefits. The game's fast-paced nature demands quick thinking and constant mental alertness, which can enhance cognitive functions. Planning strategies, recalling scores, and adapting to opponents' playing styles keep the brain active and engaged, potentially staving off the cognitive decline that sometimes accompanies aging. The hand-eye coordination required also sharpens reflexes, providing a wholesome brain workout every time a senior steps onto the court.

However, to make pickleball a safe and enjoyable experience for seniors, certain adaptations might be necessary. Recognizing that seniors may have varying levels of mobility and physical strength, using lighter paddles can make the game much easier and more enjoyable. These paddles reduce the strain on joints and muscles, making it easier to play longer without fatigue. Considering softer balls can also be a wise choice, as they are easier to hit and less likely to cause injuries. Additionally, modifying the court size, perhaps by shortening the width or length, can make the game more accessible by reducing the amount of movement required to play effectively.

The social aspect of pickleball is one of its most significant benefits, particularly for seniors. Regular play can strengthen community ties, providing a social outlet many older adults miss, especially after retirement. The game naturally fosters interaction and camaraderie, as players often gather in groups, share strategies, and engage in friendly competition. This socialization can be instrumental in reducing feelings of isolation and loneliness, which are significant factors in senior health and well-being. The laughter, encouragement, and companionship found on the pickleball courts can uplift spirits and contribute to overall mental health.

Organizing pickleball activities for seniors requires thoughtful consideration to ensure that everyone feels welcome and engaged. Planning sessions during cooler times, such as early mornings or late afternoons, can make playing more comfortable, especially in warmer climates. Ensuring adequate hydration stations and shaded rest areas can help manage energy levels and prevent heat exhaustion. It's also beneficial to structure sessions with plenty of breaks and varying levels of play, allowing seniors to engage at their own pace without feeling pressured or overly fatigued.

By embracing these adaptations and considerations, pickleball can become an excellent activity for seniors as a form of physical exercise and a vibrant social activity that enriches their lives. The integration of these elements—health benefits, safety adaptations, and community building—makes pickleball an ideal sport for seniors, offering them a pathway to improved wellness and joyful engagement with peers.

As this chapter closes, we reflect on the vibrant tapestry of opportunities pickleball offers to players across the age spectrum. From the energetic dashes of children to the strategic plays of seniors, pickleball is more than just a game; it is a conduit for health, joy, and community. Moving forward, the next chapter will delve into the essential strategies for safety and injury prevention, making sure that everyone, regardless of age or skill set, can enjoy the benefits of pickleball in a safe and supportive environment.

SAFETY AND INJURY PREVENTION

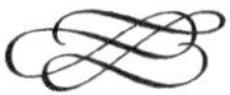

Picture this: You're stepping onto the pickleball court, the sun is shining, and you're ready for a game that's as enjoyable as it is invigorating. Now, imagine enhancing that experience by knowing you're fully prepped to play your best game, free from the worry of injuries or discomfort. That's what this chapter is all about—ensuring your pickleball outings are not just fun but also safe and conducive to your long-term wellness. Think of this as your playbook for keeping the game light, limber, and leisurely so every step on the court is as safe as it is enjoyable.

8.1 WARM-UPS AND COOL-DOWNS

The Importance of Dynamic Warm-Ups

Before you launch into the heart of the game, a good warm-up session is as essential as your paddle and shoes. Why, you ask? Doing dynamic stretching and light aerobic activities before you play is like giving your muscles a heads-up. A dynamic warm-up incorporates movements specific to the motions you'll be performing during your game. These movements prepare your body for physical activity by increasing heart rate, blood flow, and muscle temperature. A dynamic warm-up involves active movements that take your muscles and joints through a full range of motion.

Sample Warm-Up Routine

Let's dive into a specific 10-minute warm-up routine tailored for pickleball. This routine will prepare your body for the quick starts, stops, and agile movements the game demands. Start with about three minutes of gentle jogging or brisk walking. This initial step helps increase your heart rate and blood circulation, gently prepping your body for more vigorous activities.

Next, spend about two minutes on arm circles—With both arms held straight out to the sides, begin making small circles that gradually increase to larger circles. This movement helps loosen up the shoulders, which are crucial for those powerful serves and volleys. Follow this with leg swings for another two minutes. Hold onto something stable for support, and swing one leg forward and backward. This exercise warms up your hip flexors, quadriceps, and hamstrings, which are heavily involved in moving around the court and lunging for the ball.

Cool-Down Benefits

After the game, it's tempting to pack up and head home, but incorporating a cool-down routine can be just as beneficial as your pre-game warm-up. Cooling down allows your body to slowly return to a resting state, preventing muscle stiffness and soreness, which can be a real spoiler if you're playing multiple days in a row. It also helps with quicker recovery, reducing the lactic acid build-up in your muscles, which often causes soreness.

Cool-Down Exercises

Here's a sequence of cool-down stretches focusing on areas that are typically taxed during a pickleball game. Begin with calf stretches—stand facing a wall with one foot in front of the other and lean forward while keeping your back heel on the ground. Hold for about 30 seconds for each leg.

Follow this with hamstring stretches. Sit on the ground and extend one leg out. Use both arms to reach toward your toes while keeping your back straight. Hold this position for 30 seconds per leg.

Next, stretch your shoulders by bringing one arm across your body and lightly pulling it closer with the other arm, holding for about 30 seconds on each side.

Finish your cool-down with some gentle back stretches. Lie down on your back, bring your knees to your chest, and gently rock side to side. This helps relieve tension in your lower back, which is especially important given the quick turns and bends during the game

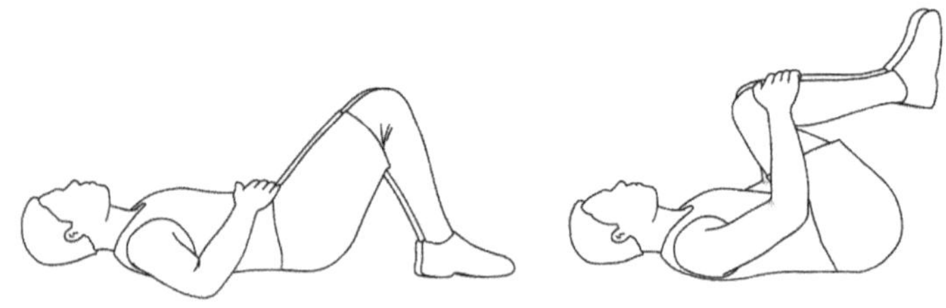

By integrating these warm-ups and cool-downs into your pickleball routine, you're not just prepping for a safer game but also enhancing your overall playing experience, ensuring that every

game is as enjoyable as it is safe. Now, with your muscles warmed up and later cooled down, you're not just ready to play; you're prepared to play your best, safely and effectively.

8.2 COMMON INJURIES AND HOW TO AVOID THEM

When fully immersed in the excitement of a pickleball game, it's easy to forget that every swift move and sudden stop carries a risk of injury. Understanding the common injuries in pickleball and how to prevent them can make your playtime enjoyable and safer. Let's look at some typical injuries that might occur on the court. Ankle sprains are at the top of the list; they happen when you make a rapid, twisting motion with your foot planted on the ground, which can stretch or tear the ligaments around your ankle. Knee injuries, including tears in the meniscus or ACL, can occur from sudden direction changes or from improper jumping and landing. Muscle strains are also common and can happen in any muscle, but the calves, hamstrings, and back are particularly susceptible due to the quick starts and stops in the game.

Each of these injuries has tell-tale signs and symptoms. Ankle sprains may cause immediate swelling, pain, and a range of motion that is painful or limited. Knee injuries might result in a popping sensation, followed by severe pain and swelling, difficulty walking, or instability in the knee. Muscle strains often cause sudden muscle pain, tenderness, swelling, and loss of muscle strength or flexibility. Recognizing these symptoms early can help manage the injury more effectively and prevent further damage.

Preventing these injuries starts with adopting the proper techniques. For instance, learning how to pivot and change direction can protect your knees and ankles from harmful twisting motions. Routine strength training and flexibility exercises can also reduce your risk of muscle strains by improving the overall condition of your muscles and joints, making them more resilient to the stresses of the game. It's also crucial to listen to your body and recognize signs of fatigue and overuse. Overexerting yourself or ignoring pain can turn minor issues into major injuries, so taking regular breaks and pacing yourself during play is essential.

Another critical aspect of injury prevention is wearing the proper footwear. Pickleball can be played on various surfaces, from gym floors to concrete and even grass, and each type of court has different traction and impact characteristics. Shoes that provide sufficient support and have good traction appropriate for the surface you're playing on can significantly reduce the risk of falls and related injuries. Look for shoes with lateral support to protect against ankle rolls, and consider cushioned soles to minimize the impact on your joints, especially if you're playing on hard surfaces.

Lastly, injuries can still occur despite all precautions, and knowing how to handle them is crucial. The RICE method—rest, ice, compression, and elevation—is often effective for minor injuries like mild ankle sprains or muscle strains. Resting prevents further strain, ice reduces swelling, compression helps minimize swelling and provides support, and elevation decreases swelling. These steps can be crucial for quick recovery. However, it's important to consult a healthcare professional if you're in severe pain, can't bear weight on the area, or if swelling and pain don't improve with home treatment.

By incorporating these preventive strategies into your pickleball routine, you're not just gearing up for a safer game but also enhancing your overall playing longevity. Acknowledging the risks and preparing accordingly helps keep you active on the court and out of the doctor's office, letting you enjoy every game to its fullest, with peace of mind that you're taking the best care of your body.

8.3 SAFETY GEAR

When you think about stepping onto the pickleball court, safety gear might not be the first thing that pops into your mind. But just like the paddle in your hand or the shoes on your feet, the proper safety equipment plays a pivotal role in ensuring that your game is fun and safe. Protective eyewear, gloves, and knee pads are essential tools that shield you from common injuries, allowing you to enjoy the game with peace of mind.

Starting with protective eyewear, it's crucial to shield your eyes during play. The risk of injury is there, whether it's a misfired ball or an accidental paddle swing. When selecting eyewear, look for lenses with UV protection to safeguard your eyes from harmful ultraviolet rays during outdoor play. This is especially important during long matches under the sun. Additionally, opt for anti-fog lenses to maintain clear vision throughout the game. There's nothing more frustrating than having your eyewear fog up in the middle of an intense rally. Shatterproof lenses made of polycarbonate can prevent serious injuries if the glasses are struck by a ball or paddle, providing robust protection without sacrificing clarity or comfort.

Moving on to gloves, you might wonder how they fit into the pickleball ensemble. Gloves are not just for cold weather; they provide a firm grip on your paddle, which is crucial for controlling your shots, especially when sweating. More importantly, many gloves come padded on the palms and fingers, offering an extra layer of cushioning in case of a fall. This padding can absorb some of the impacts, protecting your hands from scrapes and bruises, which are common in fast-paced games. Moreover, gloves can help prevent blisters from forming during extended playing sessions, keeping your hands ready and comfortable game after game.

Knee pads might seem a bit much until you've had a few close encounters with the court surface during a vigorous game. They are particularly valuable on harder court surfaces, where a fall can result in painful knee injuries. Knee pads provide not just cushioning upon impact but also valuable peace of mind, allowing you to dive for that seemingly unreachable shot without fear. The confidence to reach further and play harder can often be the edge you need to excel in your game.

Finally, customizing your safety gear for the best fit and protection is crucial. Everyone's body is different, and what works for one player might not be ideal for another. When choosing safety gear, consider your own needs and comfort preferences. For instance, adjustable straps on knee pads can ensure a snug fit that keeps the pads in place without cutting off circulation. For eyewear, look for frames that match the shape of your face, and ensure they have a secure but comfortable fit to prevent them from sliding during play. Trying on different gear and consulting with more experienced players can provide insights into what works best for you, ensuring that each piece of equipment enhances your safety without compromising your comfort or performance on the court.

By integrating these pieces of safety gear into your pickleball routine, you protect yourself from potential injuries and enhance your overall playing experience. Each item, from eyewear to knee pads, adds a layer of security that lets you focus on the game, knowing you're well protected against the common risks of the sport. Now, as you gear up with the proper safety equipment, you're not just prepared to play; you're prepared to play it safely and enjoy every moment on the court.

Remember that taking proactive steps to protect yourself plays a crucial role in your pickleball experience. It's about more than just avoiding injuries; it's about embracing a lifestyle that values well-being and enjoyment in every game. Armed with the proper techniques and gear, you're set to play and thrive on the court. Looking ahead, the next chapter will explore the exciting world of pickleball equipment, diving deeper into how choosing the right paddle, ball, and more can improve your performance and enjoyment of the game.

EQUIPMENT DEEP DIVE

Imagine stepping onto the pickleball court, paddle in hand, feeling that perfect balance and comfort that seems almost tailored to your grip. This chapter is all about deep diving into the world of pickleball equipment, focusing particularly on paddles—your primary tool in the game. A well-selected paddle can feel like an extension of your arm, enhancing your performance and enjoyment of the game. Whether you're a novice just starting or an experienced player refining your skills, understanding the nuances of paddle technology and design can significantly impact your game strategy and style.

9.1 ADVANCED PADDLE SELECTION

When selecting the right paddle, the material, design, and construction play pivotal roles in how the paddle performs in your hand. Let's explore the sophisticated world of paddle materials—graphite, composite, and carbon fiber. Each material offers unique benefits, affecting paddle stiffness, power, and control. Graphite paddles are known for their lightweight and stiff nature, offering quick action and precise ball control, making them a favorite among players who value speed and accuracy. Composite paddles, on the other hand, are generally made from a blend of materials, including fiberglass. They provide a good middle ground with moderate weight and offer excellent power, making them versatile for aggressive smashes and controlled shots. Carbon fiber paddles represent the high-end paddle technology, offering superior strength and stiffness with minimal weight, allowing for powerful shots without the fatigue associated with heavier paddles.

Moving on to the paddle's edge guard and surface texture—these are not just functional elements but can significantly influence your game. The edge guard serves as a protective barrier around the paddle, preventing damage during play. When examining paddles, look for an edge guard that is durable but not overly bulky, as a heavy guard can affect the balance and feel of the paddle. The surface texture of the paddle impacts how the ball interacts with the paddle, affecting spin and speed. A textured surface can grip the ball better, allowing for more spin and control in your shots. When selecting a paddle, consider how the texture feels and whether it complements your style of play, whether you're aiming for more spin or prefer a smoother, faster interaction with the ball.

The core of the paddle is where a lot of the magic happens. The most common core materials are polymer, Nomex, and aluminum, each affecting the paddle's overall feel and sound differently. Polymer cores are known for their soft, controlled feel, making them ideal for players who prefer a quieter game with plenty of ball control. Nomex cores are denser and harder, offering more power and a louder pop on impact, and are suited for players who like a fast, aggressive game. Aluminum cores strike a balance with moderate touch and sound, providing a good blend of power and control, suitable for players who enjoy a versatile play style.

Lastly, a paddle's weight distribution and handle design can significantly affect its maneuverability and comfort. A well-balanced paddle can enhance your swing speed and reduce strain on your arm, allowing longer play with less fatigue. The handle design is crucial for comfort; it should fit well in your hand, with an ergonomic grip that prevents slipping and reduces the risk of blisters. When testing paddles, pay attention to how the paddle feels in your swing—does it feel top-heavy, or is the weight evenly distributed? How does the grip feel after several swings? These factors can significantly influence your comfort and performance on the court.

By taking the time to understand these advanced aspects of paddle selection, you equip yourself with the knowledge to choose a paddle that not only fits your physical needs but also complements your playing style. Whether enjoying a friendly match or facing off in a tournament, the right paddle can make all the difference, turning a good game into a great one.

9.2 ADVANCED BALL SELECTION

When you step onto the pickleball court, the ball you choose can be as crucial as your paddle. Not all pickleball balls are created equal, and understanding the nuances of ball construction and durability can significantly enhance your game. Let's talk about what makes a high-performance pickleball ball. Typically, these balls are crafted from a robust, hard plastic designed to withstand the rigors of fast-paced play. The number of holes in a ball can vary, usually ranging from 26 to

40, and these holes are strategically designed to influence the ball's flight path and speed. A higher number of holes can increase the ball's air resistance, slowing it down during play. It can be particularly useful in windy conditions or when precision is more critical than power. The quality of the plastic also plays a significant role in how long the ball lasts and how consistently it performs. High-quality plastic withstands hits and maintains its shape and texture over time, ensuring the ball's performance doesn't degrade after repeated games.

Environmental factors also play a significant role in how a pickleball behaves during play. Temperature and humidity can affect the ball's hardness and weight, influencing its bounce and flight speed. In cooler temperatures, balls become harder and less bouncy, which might affect your playing style, primarily if you rely on a bouncier ball to execute your strategies. Conversely, in warmer climates, balls can soften, providing a higher bounce and potentially altering the trajectory of your shots. Humidity can make the balls heavier and slower, which might require adjusting your power and spin to maintain control. When selecting balls for different environments, consider these factors carefully. Opt for a ball that consistently performs in the climate you typically play in, ensuring your game remains steady regardless of the weather.

The distinction between indoor and outdoor pickleball balls is another crucial consideration. Balls designed for indoor play are generally lighter and softer, with larger holes to adapt to smoother, less abrasive indoor court surfaces. This design helps the ball move slower, allowing for more reaction time, perfect for tight indoor spaces. Outdoor balls, in contrast, are made to be tougher. They are heavier and have smaller, more tightly spaced holes. This construction helps them withstand rougher, textured court surfaces and reduces the impact of wind on the ball's path. Consider where you most often play when choosing between indoor and outdoor balls. Using the correct type of ball for your environment ensures optimal performance and reduces the wear on the ball, giving you a better playing experience.

Customizing your pickleball balls can be a game-changer for those seeking a competitive edge. Customization options like choosing different colors can vastly improve visibility against various court surfaces, enhancing your reaction time and accuracy. Some players prefer balls with specific weights and hardness to suit their playing style, with heavier balls providing more power and lighter balls offering more control. Experimenting with these customizations can help you find the perfect ball that matches your personal preferences and complements your strategy, giving you an advantage in competitive play.

By thoroughly considering the construction, environmental suitability, and customization of your pickleball balls, you equip yourself with the knowledge to choose the best ball for your games. Whether practicing or competing, the right ball can make all the difference, transforming how you play and enjoy pickleball.

9.3 HIGH-PERFORMANCE FOOTWEAR

When you're gearing up for a game of pickleball, the importance of choosing the proper footwear cannot be overstressed. Just like the right paddle can enhance your control and power, the right shoes can drastically improve your mobility and stability on the court. Let's delve into why the durability of the sole and its traction patterns are crucial for your performance. The soles of your shoes are your foundation during play, facing constant friction against the court surface with every swift move or sudden stop. Durable soles ensure that your shoes withstand this wear over time, maintaining their structure and functionality. More importantly, the traction pattern on these soles plays a crucial role in your ability to move swiftly and safely. Adequate grip helps prevent slips and falls, especially during fast-paced games, and aids in making those quick, agile movements that pickleball often demands. Look for soles that match the typical court surfaces you play on, whether a herringbone pattern for hard courts or larger, flatter treads for softer surfaces.

Navigating the trade-offs between lightweight and heavier footwear is another aspect that significantly influences your game. Lighter shoes can enhance your speed, making it easier to move quickly and effortlessly across the court. They allow for rapid directional changes without the burden of extra weight, ideal for players who rely on their speed and agility. However, lighter shoes might offer little stability and cushioning, which is crucial for maintaining balance and absorbing shocks during play. On the other hand, heavier shoes usually provide better stability and support. They can help anchor your movements, which is particularly beneficial if your playing style involves a lot of powerful strokes that require a firm base. The extra weight could slow you down, so it's about finding the right balance that completes your specific needs and playing style.

Recent innovations in shoe technology have vastly improved player comfort and support on the court. Modern pickleball shoes have various features designed to maximize comfort and minimize injury risks. Enhanced cushioning systems in the sole can absorb impact better, protecting your joints during those intense plays. Arch support is crucial, especially for players who spend hours on the court, as it prevents overpronation and reduces the risk of developing plantar fasciitis. Breathable materials used in shoe construction keep your feet dry and prevent bacterial growth from sweat. When trying on pickleball shoes, pay attention to how these features feel and whether they provide the support and comfort you need for your style of play.

Choosing the proper footwear based on the court surface you frequently play on can further optimize your performance. Different surfaces impact how the game is played and, by extension, what demands are placed on your footwear. For example, playing on textured concrete requires shoes with excellent grip and durability to handle the rough surface without wearing out quickly. Composite surfaces, like those found in many modern sports facilities, might call for shoes with more cushioning to deal with the harder impact. Softer gym floors need shoes with less intense tread patterns to avoid damaging the floor and provide enough grip without sticking too much. Always consider where you'll be playing most of your games when selecting your shoes, as the right choice can enhance your performance while ensuring your shoes last longer.

Reflection Section: Evaluate Your Current Footwear

Take a moment to evaluate your current pickleball footwear. Consider its condition, how well it meets your needs, and whether it's suited to the surfaces you play on most often. Reflect on whether your shoes could contribute to any discomfort or performance issues you've experienced recently.

As we wrap up this chapter on high-performance footwear, remember that the right shoes are as crucial as any piece of equipment in your pickleball arsenal. They affect how you play and can prevent injuries and enhance your overall playing experience. With this knowledge, you're better equipped to choose footwear that feels great and elevates your game, allowing you to play with confidence and comfort, no matter where your pickleball adventures take you.

PICKLEBALL RULES AND ETIQUETTE

Stepping onto the pickleball court, you're not just entering a space to play; you're stepping into a world guided by rules that ensure fairness, safety, and enjoyment for everyone involved. In 2023, some of these rules have evolved, reflecting the sport's growing sophistication and global reach. Understanding these changes isn't just about keeping up; it's about deepening your appreciation of pickleball and refining your skills and strategies to align with today's best practices.

10.1 2023 RULE CHANGES

Detailed Breakdown of New Rules

The landscape of pickleball has seen some exciting changes in 2023 aimed at improving the experience and safety of all players. One notable update is the adjustment to the serve rules. Previously, the ball had to be hit below the waist level at a downward angle. The new rule allows for more flexibility;

permitting serves to be struck below the chest level. This change aims to accommodate players of various heights and playing styles, making the serve a more strategic and accessible part of the game.

Another significant update is the introduction of a fault margin for service line violations. Instead of an immediate fault, players have a margin of error of up to two inches over the line before a fault is called. This adjustment acknowledges minor foot placement errors that may not provide a competitive advantage, thus keeping the game flowing more smoothly.

The double-bounce rule, which requires the ball to bounce once on each side before volleys are allowed, has been refined to clarify situations where the ball spins or rolls back over the net to the other side. In such cases, players are now permitted to cross over the net to hit the ball, provided they do not touch the net or the opponent's court. This update addresses rare but tricky situations, ensuring that play can continue fairly and without confusion.

Rationale Behind Changes

The rationale for these updates is rooted in the core principles of pickleball: fairness, safety, and enjoyment. By adjusting the serve rules, the governing bodies aim to level the playing field, giving players of all heights and abilities the chance to serve effectively and competitively. The introduction of a fault margin for line violations reduces unnecessary interruptions and disputes over minor infractions that don't significantly impact the game's outcome.

The clarification of the double-bounce rule enhances safety by allowing players to handle unusual plays without risking a collision at the net. These changes reflect a nuanced understanding of the game's dynamics and a commitment to continuous improvement, ensuring pickleball remains as engaging and inclusive as possible.

Adjusting Gameplay to New Rules

Adapting to new rules requires both mental and physical adjustments. For the updated serve rules, consider practicing serves at different heights within the new legal range, experimenting with what works best for your style while staying within the updated guidelines. Incorporating drills focusing on precision and control can help you maximize the new serving flexibility.

The line violation margin is a good opportunity to become more aware of your positioning during serves. Practice serves where you consciously place your feet just behind the line, ensuring you're consistently within the legal bounds and thus avoiding faults during critical points in a match.

Official Sources and Further Reading

To fully embrace these changes and understand their nuances, it's crucial to consult official sources. The USA Pickleball Association (USAPA) provides comprehensive resources, including updated rulebooks and detailed interpretations that help clarify how these rules should be applied in various scenarios. Engaging with these materials keeps you informed and enhances your strategic approach to the game.

10.2 LINE CALLS AND DISPUTES

Making fair and accurate line calls is a fundamental part of pickleball that respects the integrity of the game and maintains its spirit of fair competition. When you're on the court, you are responsible for making line calls on your side. This can sometimes feel daunting, but with the right approach, you can make calls confidently and fairly. Firstly, positioning is crucial. You should be in a spot where you can clearly see the line; this often means staying parallel whenever possible. Keeping your focus during points is equally important. It's easy to get caught up in the excitement of the game, but maintaining concentration on where the ball lands can make all the difference in making an accurate call.

Sometimes, even with the best intentions and focus, the ball moves too fast or lands too close to the line to call confidently. In these instances, giving your opponent the benefit of the doubt upholds the sportsmanship spirit of pickleball. If you're unsure, it's generally better to call it in favor of the opponent. This approach fosters a friendly game environment and respects the principle that pickleball is a game meant to be enjoyed by all, regardless of the competitive heat.

Handling disputes over line calls or rules gracefully is just as important as the initial call.

Disagreements can arise, but how you handle these moments can define the game's enjoyment for everyone involved. The first step in a dispute is to communicate clearly and calmly. State your perspective respectfully and listen to your opponent's viewpoint. More often than not, a calm discussion can resolve the difference. However, maintaining composure becomes your most powerful tool if the disagreement persists. Getting visibly upset or angry only escalates the tension, which can detract from the game's enjoyment.

There are times when resolving a dispute amicably between players isn't possible. In these cases, involving a third party or a referee is wise. Referees are trained to handle such conflicts objectively. Their role is to assess the situation impartially and make a call based on the rules of pickleball. If you find yourself in a situation where a referee needs to be involved, it's essential to respect their decision, whether it favors you or not. They provide their judgment based on their perspective and understanding of the rules, aiming to ensure that the game is played fairly.

Above all, remember that sportsmanship should always come before a competitive edge. Prioritizing fair play and mutual respect over winning at all costs makes the game more enjoyable and honors the spirit in which pickleball was created. It's about more than just playing by the rules; it's about valuing the experience and the people you share the court with. This ethos should guide every serve, every volley, and every line call, ensuring that pickleball remains a sport beloved for its friendly competition and community spirit.

10.3 ETIQUETTE AND SPORTSMANSHIP

Understanding the fundamentals of good sportsmanship in pickleball goes beyond the game's basic rules; it taps into the heart of why we play sports—to connect with others, challenge ourselves, and enjoy healthy competition. Good sportsmanship is demonstrated through actions such as shaking hands with your opponent before and after matches. This gesture, though small, signifies respect for each other as players and appreciation for the opportunity to play together. Complimenting opponents on good plays also fosters a spirit of respect. It shows acknowledgment of their skills and effort, which can significantly uplift the game's atmosphere, making the competition fierce but friendly.

Respecting officials and accepting their calls without contention is another cornerstone of good sportsmanship. Officials work hard to ensure the game is played fairly, and showing them respect, even when you disagree with a call, sets a positive example for everyone on the court. These behaviors collectively uphold the integrity of the game and ensure that it remains enjoyable for all participants.

The etiquette expected on the court extends to both players and spectators. For players, it's essential to maintain a level of decorum that includes keeping noise to a minimum during play. This shows respect for your opponent's concentration and enhances your focus. Additionally, players should avoid walking through courts while a game is in progress. This disrupts the game's flow and can also be a safety hazard. Respecting the playing area and the equipment used during games is crucial; treat paddles, balls, and the net with care, as these are the tools of the sport that everyone shares.

While not directly involved in the gameplay, spectators play a significant role in creating the game's atmosphere. They should also adhere to etiquette guidelines, such as staying quiet during rallies and clapping or cheering at appropriate times. Encouraging positive and respectful cheering enhances the enjoyment for players and spectators, creating an environment where everyone feels supported and valued.

Promoting positive interactions during play is vital to ensuring that pickleball remains a sport enjoyed by people of all ages and skill levels. Players can foster a positive environment by consistently encouraging their teammates and opponents. This can be as simple as a thumbs-up for a good shot or offering encouragement after a tough point. Handling winning and losing with grace is equally important. Celebrate your victories with humility and accept defeats with dignity, taking them as opportunities to learn and improve. Being a good role model, especially for younger players or those new to the sport, involves demonstrating these values consistently. Your behavior can inspire others to adopt the same attitudes, strengthening the community spirit inherent in pickleball.

Community involvement and leadership are pivotal in promoting sportsmanship and etiquette within the pickleball community. Experienced players can act as role models and mentors for newer players, guiding them in improving their technical skills and understanding the importance of good sportsmanship. Volunteering in local leagues or tournaments is a great way to give back to the community that supports your playing activities. By helping organize events, officiate games, or provide coaching, you help create a structured, positive environment where players can thrive.

This active participation enriches your experience and contributes to the pickleball community's growth and positive culture. It's about putting into practice the values of respect, fairness, and enjoyment that make pickleball such a beloved sport. As you continue to engage with the community, whether through playing, spectating, or organizing, remember that your actions on and off the court can inspire others and shape the future of pickleball.

As we close this chapter on etiquette and sportsmanship, reflect on how these principles impact your individual games and the broader pickleball community. Carrying forward these values ensures that pickleball remains an enriching and enjoyable experience for everyone involved. Looking ahead, we will explore the exciting world of indoor versus outdoor play, providing you with insights to maximize your game in any setting.

INDOOR VS. OUTDOOR

11.1 INDOOR GAME ENVIRONMENT

As you step into the echoing buzz of an indoor pickleball court, it's like entering a different world—where elements such as wind and sunlight are replaced by the hum of overhead lights and the distinctive sound of pickleball balls bouncing off hard surfaces. Playing pickleball indoors offers unique conditions and challenges that can significantly influence your game strategy and performance. Let's explore how to adapt and thrive in this controlled yet dynamic environment.

Understanding Indoor Court Dynamics

Indoor pickleball courts often feature artificial lighting and lack natural elements like wind, affecting how you perceive and react to the ball. The controlled lighting reduces variables, allowing for more consistent visibility than outdoor play, where shadows or glaring sun can interfere with your sight.

However, the intensity or uneven distribution of artificial light might require adjusting how you track the ball during play.

The absence of wind indoors is a double-edged sword. On one hand, it offers a stable environment where the ball travels smoothly and predictably, allowing you to execute precise shots and serves without the need to compensate for gusts or breezes. This stability often leads to faster-paced games, as players can aggressively attack the ball with confidence that it will go precisely where intended. On the other hand, the lack of wind assistance means you'll need to rely purely on your power and technique to drive the ball deep into the opponent's court or to finesse it gently over the net.

Indoor courts are typically smaller than their outdoor counterparts, or they may be sectioned off within larger gym spaces, leading to variations in court size and boundary lines. This can affect your spatial strategy, as you have less room to maneuver or different angles to consider when placing your shots. The compact space accelerates gameplay, requiring quick reflexes and anticipatory skills to handle the rapid exchanges at the net.

Strategies for Indoor Play

Adapting your play style to the unique conditions of indoor pickleball can give you a competitive edge. One effective strategy is to use the walls and ceiling within legal play boundaries. In some indoor facilities, balls that hit the ceiling or specific wall areas are still in play, creating unexpected opportunities to keep the rally going or catch your opponent off guard. Familiarize yourself with the local rules regarding these scenarios and practice shots that take advantage of vertical plays when possible.

Adjusting your serving technique can also be beneficial in an indoor setting. With lower ceilings or shorter court lengths, a high-arcing serve might be less effective or even risk hitting the ceiling. Instead, focus on mastering a low, fast serve that skims just over the net, minimizing the chance of ceiling interference and maximizing the speed and unpredictability of your serve to challenge your opponent.

Noise Factors and Communication

Indoor courts often amplify sounds, from the pop of the pickleball on your paddle to the general buzz of players and spectators. This heightened noise level can be distracting, making it difficult to hear calls from your partner or referee. To combat this, prioritize clear and concise verbal communication during play. Establish simple, loud call-outs for "mine," "yours," or "out," and consider using hand signals as a supplementary communication method, especially if the acoustic environment makes verbal communication challenging.

Adapting to Surface Types

Indoor pickleball courts can vary significantly in surface type, from wooden gym floors to synthetic mats or even carpeted surfaces. Each type presents different challenges in terms of traction and ball bounce. On wooden or synthetic floors, you may experience more slide, requiring shoes with good grip and lateral support to prevent slips and falls. While less common, carpeted surfaces can cause the ball to slow down or bounce unpredictably, necessitating quicker footwork and more reactive shot adjustments.

Choose footwear that matches the court surface to enhance your stability and performance when playing indoors. For wooden and synthetic surfaces, look for shoes with enhanced grip and sufficient cushioning to absorb the impact of quick movements. If you frequently play on different surfaces, consider investing in a few pairs of shoes suited to each condition, ensuring you're always prepared to play your best, no matter where you are.

As you continue to play and familiarize yourself with the nuances of indoor pickleball, you'll find that each court brings unique challenges and advantages. Embrace these differences, adapt your strategies accordingly, and enjoy the dynamic, fast-paced game that indoor pickleball offers.

11.2 OUTDOOR GAME ENVIRONMENT

Playing pickleball outdoors introduces a delightful dimension to the game that includes fresh air and natural light. However, it also brings variables like wind, sun, and temperature changes, each impacting your gameplay uniquely. Adapting to these conditions enhances your comfort and can become a strategic advantage if you know how to use them to your benefit. For instance, wind can be a tricky factor to contend with, but with the right approach, it can also aid your play. When you're facing the wind, it's your ally for adding extra speed to your serves and returns, forcing your opponents to adjust their timing and strategy. Conversely, a softer touch on your shots can prevent them from sailing out of bounds when playing with the wind at your back. This adjustment requires practice, as the wind's intensity can vary, but once mastered, it allows you to control the game's pace more effectively.

Sun glare is another outdoor challenge, particularly during morning or late afternoon games when the sun is low. Positioning yourself so the sun is behind you can minimize its impact on your visibility and prevent it from becoming a distraction. Wearing a cap or sunglasses specifically designed for sports can also help manage the glare, ensuring you don't lose sight of the ball during critical plays. Additionally, paying attention to the sun's position throughout the game and adjusting your position accordingly can keep you at a visual advantage over your opponent.

Temperature fluctuations present another aspect of outdoor play that requires consideration. In warmer conditions, the ball tends to fly faster and bounce higher, which might alter the way you approach your shots and serves. Cooler weather, conversely, can make the ball harder and less responsive, necessitating a more forceful playing style to maintain your usual game pace. Adapting your strategy to these conditions means being observant and flexible, adjusting your force and tactics as the temperature dictates.

Maintaining focus amidst the varying conditions of outdoor play is crucial and can be managed through a combination of preparation and practice. The distractions of a public park or beach—like background noise from spectators or nearby activities—can be mitigated by developing a routine that helps you stay focused. This might involve specific breathing techniques or a set of pre-point rituals that help you reset and refocus between rallies. Regular practice in different outdoor environments also equips you with the experience to remain unfazed by unexpected noises or interruptions, keeping your performance steady regardless of external distractions.

Choosing the proper ball is paramount when it comes to equipment suitable for outdoor conditions. Outdoor pickleball balls are specifically designed to handle the wind and hard court surfaces. They are typically harder and have smaller, more tightly spaced holes compared to indoor balls, which helps reduce the wind's influence on the ball's trajectory and ensures a consistent bounce on harder surfaces. Using the correct type of ball for outdoor conditions improves game quality and prevents the wear and tear that indoor balls might suffer when used outside.

Finally, safeguarding your health and safety during outdoor play cannot be overstressed. Always ensure you are well-hydrated, and make it a point to drink fluids regularly throughout your play, not just when you feel thirsty. Applying broad-spectrum sunscreen to protect against UV rays, wearing appropriate protective clothing like light, breathable fabrics that cover exposed skin, and sunglasses are all essential to guard against sun damage. Additionally, being aware of signs of heat exhaustion—such as excessive sweating, dizziness, and muscle cramps—is crucial, especially during intense play or in very hot conditions. Conversely, wearing layers that you can remove as you warm up helps maintain body temperature and comfort in cooler weather.

Playing pickleball outdoors offers a refreshing variation to the indoor game, filled with its unique challenges and joys. By learning to adapt to the elements and maintaining your focus, you ensure that each game is as rewarding as it is enjoyable. Whether it's a breezy day or a sunny afternoon, each outdoor match is an opportunity to refine your skills and strategies, making you a more versatile and resilient player.

11.3 EQUIPMENT CONSIDERATIONS: INDOOR VS OUTDOOR

Navigating the world of pickleball equipment can feel like being a chef selecting the perfect ingredients for a recipe. Each choice, from balls to paddles to footwear, influences the outcome of your game, especially when transitioning between indoor and outdoor environments. Understanding these differences ensures that you perform your best and enjoy the game to its fullest, whether you're playing under a roof or under the sky.

Ball Selection for Different Environments

Pickleball balls are designed for indoor or outdoor settings, each tailored to optimize performance and durability under specific conditions. Indoor balls are generally softer and lighter, crafted from smoother plastic, which gives them a slightly bouncy character on indoor surfaces. They typically feature larger holes, which slow the ball down in the air, making them easier to hit in a controlled, less windy environment. This design suits the typically shorter court dimensions and the faster game pace indoors, where reactions must be quick and precise.

Outdoor balls, in contrast, are built to endure the harsher conditions of outdoor play. Made from a harder plastic, they are heavier, which helps them move predictively in the wind and resist deformation. The smaller, more tightly spaced holes minimize the effects of wind, providing a stable and more predictable flight path. This durability is crucial for dealing with rougher surfaces like concrete or asphalt, which can rapidly wear down a softer indoor ball. When choosing balls for either setting, consider how these characteristics align with your play style and the conditions you expect to encounter. A well-chosen ball can elevate your game, ensuring that your skills are showcased no matter the venue.

Paddle Characteristics for Indoor/Outdoor Play

As with balls, the choice of paddle can significantly influence your game in different environments. When playing indoors, where the game is faster, and the ball is lighter, a lighter paddle can provide the quick response and speed needed for rapid volleys and fast exchanges. The surface texture of the paddle also plays a significant role; a smoother surface may offer better control and less spin, ideal for the quick, precise game typical of indoor play.

For outdoor play, where conditions can be more variable and the ball is heavier and harder, a heavier paddle can be beneficial. The additional weight provides more power behind shots, which is necessary to handle heavier balls and windy conditions. A rougher paddle surface can also help in applying more spin to the ball, an advantage when playing outdoors where the elements can alter the ball's path. This spin can counteract some of the unpredictable elements, giving you more control over your play.

Footwear Adaptations

Proper footwear is crucial in adapting to different playing surfaces, directly impacting your performance and your risk of injury. Indoor courts, often made of wood or synthetic materials, can be slick, necessitating shoes with good grip and non-marking soles to prevent slipping and to protect the court surface. These shoes should also offer good lateral support to accommodate the quick side-to-side movements typical of pickleball.

Outdoor courts can vary from concrete to composite surfaces, often rougher and more abrasive than indoor courts. Here, footwear needs thicker, more durable soles to withstand the wear and tear of rough surfaces and enhanced cushioning to absorb the greater impact of playing on harder materials. Court shoes should also be chosen for their tread patterns, allowing for good stability and grip in all weather conditions.

Additional Gear for Comfort and Performance

Other gear considerations include clothing and accessories that can help you adapt to different environments. For indoor play, moisture-wicking materials are essential to manage sweat, as indoor spaces can get warm and stuffy. These garments keep you dry and comfortable, maintaining your focus and performance.

For outdoor play, your clothing should offer protection from the elements in addition to moisture-wicking properties. Lightweight, breathable fabrics with UV protection are ideal for sunny days, while options like hats and sunglasses protect your eyes from glare and UV exposure. Layering with performance fabrics can help regulate your body temperature in cooler weather, keeping you warm without overheating as you play.

By understanding and adapting your equipment to your playing environment, you ensure that each game of pickleball is as enjoyable and successful as possible. Whether you're volleying indoors or serving outdoors, the right gear sets the stage for a great match.

As we wrap up this chapter, remember that each piece of gear, from your paddle to your shoes, plays a crucial role in how well you adapt to and perform in different environments. This knowledge prepares you for whatever conditions you face. It enriches your overall game experience, ensuring you enjoy every moment, whether playing under a roof or the open sky. Looking ahead, we'll explore more ways to enhance your pickleball skills and strategies, ensuring you're equipped with the right gear and techniques to make the most of your pickleball play.

COMPETITIVE PLAY

Stepping into your first pickleball tournament can feel like opening the door to a new adventure, where every serve, volley, and dink writes a page of your sporting saga. It's a thrilling mix of nerves, excitement, and the buzz of competition that makes all your practice sessions come to life. Whether it's the rhythmic thumping of pickleballs, the encouraging shouts from fellow players, or the sharp whistle of the referee, everything about a tournament can elevate your play and passion for the game. So, let's get you ready, from understanding the nuts and bolts of tournament play to ensuring your gear is up to par!

12.1 FIRST TOURNAMENT PREP

Understanding Tournament Structure and Rules

Pickleball tournaments can vary widely in structure, but you'll most commonly encounter single-elimination or round-robin formats. In a single-elimination setup, it's straightforward—you lose once, and you're out. This format is thrilling but ruthless, requiring you to be at your best from your first match. On the other hand, round-robin is a bit more forgiving, allowing you to play several games against multiple opponents in your group. Based on wins (and sometimes point differentials), the top performers move on to the next stage, usually culminating in a knockout phase.

Each tournament also comes with its own set of rules, which can include specific regulations about time-outs, service rotations, and how disputes are handled. Time-outs are particularly strategic, allowing you a brief respite during games to catch your breath or discuss tactics with your partner or coach. Generally, you're given one or two 60-second time-outs per game, but knowing when and how you can call them is crucial. Understanding referee interactions is also vital. Referees manage scores, enforce rules, and ensure fair play in official games. They are there to help clarify rulings and keep the game moving, so knowing how to interact with them respectfully and effectively can enhance your experience.

Pre-Tournament Preparation

The weeks leading up to a tournament allow you to fine-tune your skills and keep your body and mind primed. Physically, it's about more than just regular practice sessions. Consider incorporating interval training into your routine to mimic the burst-rest patterns in pickleball. Nutrition also plays a crucial role—fueling up on a balanced diet rich in proteins for muscle repair, carbohydrates for energy, and plenty of fluids for hydration. Don't forget the importance of sleep; a well-rested body performs significantly better, and getting those eight hours can be as crucial as any practice drill.

Prepare mentally by visualizing your matches, reviewing strategies, and setting personal goals for your performance. Mental resilience can often be the deciding factor in tight matches, so practicing stress-relief techniques and focusing on positive outcomes can keep you calm and sharp.

Equipment and Gear Check

Before the tournament, do a thorough check of all your equipment. Your paddle should be in good condition, with no damage that could affect play. Bring extra grips to change during the tournament if the old ones get worn out or slippery. Appropriate clothing is also crucial—ensure you have comfortable attire that suits the weather conditions, whether extra layers for cold mornings or moisture-wicking fabrics for hot days. Also, pack any additional gear like hats, sunglasses, or knee braces that help you play your best. It's all about feeling confident and comfortable when you step onto the court.

Scouting Competitors and Courts

If possible, arrive at the tournament venue early. This gives you a significant advantage as you can familiarize yourself with the court surfaces and conditions. Each court can have its quirks—different types of surfaces affect ball bounce and speed, and understanding these can help you adjust your game accordingly. Also, take the opportunity to watch other competitors play. Observing potential opponents can give you insights into their strategies and weaknesses, which you can discuss with your coach or partner to refine your game plan. It's about gathering all the intel you can to give yourself the best chance of success.

As you gear up for your first or next pickleball tournament, remember that preparation is as important as execution. Knowing the structure, getting your body and mind ready, ensuring your equipment is in top shape, and understanding your playing environment and competitors are all steps to not just competing, but competing to win. Dive into the challenge with enthusiasm and readiness; after all, every match is a learning experience and a step forward in your pickleball journey. As you walk onto that court, paddle in hand, remember why you started— for the love of the game, the thrill of the play, and the joy of competitive spirit. Let's make every game count!

12.2 STRATEGIES FOR SUCCESS

Adapting your play style to your opponent and the prevailing court conditions can often feel like you're a chameleon, constantly changing colors to blend perfectly with your surroundings. Imagine playing against someone with a killer backhand but struggling with low, soft shots. Here, tweaking your play to include more dink shots at their weaker forehand might just tilt the game in your favor. Similarly, the court surface plays a significant role. For instance, a lighter touch and fewer high shots on a windy day can keep the ball in play more effectively, preventing the wind from turning your game into a wild goose chase. Adjusting your serve to be less about power and more about placement can also be a game-changer under such conditions. It's about observing, adapting, and strategically manipulating the game flow to play into your strengths and exploit the weaknesses of others.

Let's talk about energy management, which is about pacing yourself to stay as fresh in your final game as you were in your first. This is where the strategic use of time-outs comes into play. Imagine you've just had a long, intense rally, and you can feel your energy draining—calling a time-out can give you those precious moments to catch your breath and refocus. Equally important is what you do during these breaks. Hydration is key, so replenish fluids and keep water or sports drinks handy. Snacking on bananas or energy bars can also provide a quick energy boost. Think of these snacks as your little pit stops—quick, efficient, and utterly essential to keep your engine running. Maintaining this balance isn't just about physical stamina; it's about keeping your mental energy up, too, so you can stay sharp and make those split-second decisions that often decide the outcome of a game.

Tactical use of scoring and momentum can often resemble a game of chess, where each move sets up the next. Understanding how to read the game's momentum and using the scoring system to your advantage is critical. Let's say you're leading, and your opponent is visibly frustrated. This is the time to play conservatively, making safe, steady shots that force them to take risks. Conversely, if you're behind, this might be the moment to try a few unexpected shots to break their rhythm and claw back into the game. It's about sensing shifts in momentum and adjusting your strategy on the fly. This dynamic approach keeps your opponents off balance and increases your chances of controlling the game's pace.

Finally, after each match, take some time to reflect on what went well and what didn't. Perhaps you aced your serves but struggled with your backhand returns. Recognizing these patterns is the first step in improving your game. Discussing these observations with a coach or a teammate can provide new insights and perspectives, helping you adjust your training focus accordingly. It could be a tweak in your serve technique or additional drills for your backhand. Each match is a learning opportunity to refine your strategies and improve your skills. This continuous cycle of performance, analysis, and adjustment elevates your game over time, turning experiences, both good and bad, into stepping stones toward becoming a more formidable and skilled pickleball player.

12.3 HANDLING PRESSURE AND EXPECTATIONS

Competitive play often comes with its share of butterflies in the stomach, and that's perfectly normal. But when nerves start taking the driver's seat, it's crucial to have techniques up your sleeve to calm them down and keep your head in the game. One effective method is deep breathing exercises, which can be a game-changer. Focusing on taking slow, deep breaths increases the oxygen flow to your brain, which helps reduce stress levels and sharpens your focus. Incorporate these exercises into your pre-game routine; try inhaling for four counts, holding for four, and exhaling for four. This calms you and gets you into a rhythm you can carry into the match.

Focused meditation is another powerful tool. Spending a few minutes meditating can center your thoughts and clear your mind of distractions. Picture yourself executing perfect shots and winning points. This visualization boosts confidence and prepares your mind to execute those visions in actual gameplay. Establishing a consistent pre-game routine that includes these practices can also instill a sense of familiarity and control, which is comforting when stepping into the unpredictable environment of a tournament.

Setting realistic goals is equally important in managing expectations and focusing your efforts. Before each tournament, define what success looks like for you. This could be as simple as improving your serve accuracy, advancing to a particular round, or even maintaining your composure under pressure. These goals should be specific, measurable, achievable, relevant, and time-bound (SMART). By focusing on these achievable objectives, you can keep your spirits high, regardless of the overall outcome. Each match becomes an opportunity to reach these mini-milestones, turning the entire experience into achievable challenges rather than an overwhelming hurdle.

Embracing a growth mindset is about seeing every match and every point as a chance to learn and grow rather than just a win or a loss. This perspective can profoundly impact your approach to the game, helping alleviate pressure by shifting the focus from fearing failure to embracing it as a learning opportunity. Whether it's a mistake that cost you a point or a loss that knocked you out of the tournament, each setback can be dissected and used as a foundation for improvement. This mindset enhances your resilience and keeps the game enjoyable and rewarding, regardless of the results.

Finally, having a solid support system in place cannot be overstated. Coaches, family members, friends, and even fellow players can provide the emotional backing you need to feel confident and supported. Their encouragement and feedback are invaluable, helping you see blind spots in your game and offering the required emotional boost to keep pushing forward.

Post-competition debriefing with your support circle is crucial; it enables you to process emotions, reflect on your performance, and plan for future improvements. This collective review can be a powerful motivator, helping you refine your strategies and mental approach for the next challenge.

Navigating the pressures and expectations of competitive play is about balance. It's about controlling your nerves, setting achievable goals, learning from every game, and leaning on your support network. These strategies aren't just about playing better pickleball—they're about enjoying the competition and growing from it, match by match.

As this chapter wraps up, remember that the pressures of competition are just as much a part of the game as the paddle and the ball. How you handle them can transform not just your performance but also your enjoyment of the game. Next, we'll explore community building within pickleball, where competition meets camaraderie, and every player can find their place and their people. Let's keep the ball rolling, finding new ways to grow both on and off the court.

BUILDING A COMMUNITY

13.1 SOCIAL BENEFITS OF CLUB MEMBERSHIP

Imagine walking onto a pickleball court, paddle in hand, greeted by familiar smiles and the friendly competition that awaits. Joining a pickleball club isn't just about playing a sport; it's about becoming part of a vibrant community that extends beyond the boundaries of the court. When you become a club member, you step into a network of enthusiasts who share your passion for pickleball, providing personal and professional networking opportunities. It's easy to form lasting friendships when you share common interests, and the regular interactions during club matches or practice sessions foster strong bonds that can last a lifetime.

Playing with a diverse group of partners and opponents is one of the quickest ways to enhance your skills. Each player, with their unique style and strategy, presents a new set of challenges and learning opportunities. For instance, playing against a more defensive opponent might teach you patience and the value of strategic placement. At the same time, an aggressive player might push you to refine your reflexes and speed. The variety keeps the game exciting and educational, ensuring you're always learning and growing. This dynamic environment, where every game is as much about learning from each other as it is about winning, helps you improve your gameplay and deepen your understanding and appreciation of pickleball.

Beyond just the games, pickleball clubs often offer a wealth of resources that can significantly enhance your playing experience. Many clubs provide access to experienced coaches who can offer personalized guidance and improve your playing techniques. Regular clinics help you stay updated on the latest strategies and rules, while club-organized tournaments can give you a taste of competitive play in a supportive environment. Moreover, clubs often have better equipment and facilities, which might otherwise be inaccessible. For example, high-quality nets, well-maintained courts, and a variety of pickleball paddles allow you to experiment and find what works best for your style of play.

The social events and activities organized by pickleball clubs are the icing on the cake. These events, ranging from casual social nights and holiday parties to more formal tournaments, provide a fun and festive atmosphere that enhances the enjoyment of the sport. For instance, a holiday-themed pickleball tournament can be a delightful event where players sport festive attire and play doubles with randomly assigned partners, adding a layer of excitement and novelty to the familiar game. These gatherings are not just about playing pickleball; they're about celebrating the community, enjoying each other's company, and making memories together on and off the court.

By joining a pickleball club, you open the door to a world of new friendships, continuous learning, and endless fun. The club becomes a second home where every match is a learning opportunity, every event is a celebration, and every member is a part of your extended pickleball family. Whether you're looking to sharpen your skills, meet new people, or enjoy the game, the club setting offers something valuable for everyone. So, take the plunge, join a club, and experience the full joy and community spirit of pickleball.

13.2 SOCIALS AND MIXERS

Organizing a pickleball social is like throwing a party where the main attractions are fun, fitness, and forging friendships. The first step in planning an event like this is choosing the right venue that accommodates both playing and socializing spaces. Ideally, look for a location with enough courts to keep games flowing and areas where attendees can relax, chat, and enjoy snacks. Creating a welcoming atmosphere where everyone feels comfortable and excited to participate is crucial. Decorations can play a big part in this—think banners, balloons, and table-cloths in bright, lively colors that reflect the energetic spirit of pickleball. When considering food, opt for light snacks that players can grab between games, such as fruits, nuts, granola bars, and plenty of water and sports drinks to keep everyone hydrated.

Music and entertainment should complement the event without overpowering it. A background playlist with upbeat, energizing music can enhance the lively vibe of a pickleball mixer without interfering with the conversations. If the budget allows, consider hiring a local DJ who can adjust the music's tempo as the event progresses from active play to more relaxed socializing. The key is to keep the energy up and ensure that the music contributes positively to the event's atmosphere.

Creativity in theming your pickleball socials can significantly boost attendance and enjoyment. For instance, a costume tournament can be a hilarious hit, with participants playing in fun and funky outfits. Imagine a doubles match where each team dresses up in coordinated costumes—superheroes, famous duos, or pickleball paddles! Another popular theme could be holiday-themed games, such as a Halloween bash where players sport costumes and play with glow-in-the-dark balls. Family days are also great, offering a mix of adult and kid-friendly activities, ensuring that everyone, regardless of age, has a good time. These themed events make the gatherings more memorable and encourage participants to engage creatively with the sport and each other.

Incorporating non-playing activities into your pickleball events ensures everyone has something to enjoy, even those who might not be playing the entire time. Setting up a picnic area with blankets and lawn games can offer a comfortable space for attendees to relax and enjoy the outdoors. Consider organizing mini-group training sessions where beginners can learn basic skills and strategies from more experienced players in a fun, informal setting. This not only helps new players get more comfortable with the game but also builds a sense of community as participants share knowledge and tips. Inviting guest speakers, such as local sports personalities or fitness experts, can provide valuable insights and introduce an educational component to the event. These speakers can talk about everything from sportsmanship and team play to nutrition and exercise, enriching the experience for all attendees.

Promotion and invitation strategies are crucial to ensure your pickleball socials are well-attended and successful. Utilizing social media platforms can generate excitement ahead of the event. Create event pages on Facebook or Instagram, share posts and updates regularly, and engage with potential attendees by answering questions and providing teasers of what they can expect. Utilizing community bulletin boards and local community groups can also help reach a wider audience. Consider designing eye-catching flyers and posters in community centers, gyms, and local businesses. Offering incentives, such as free gear rentals or prize drawings for attendees, can further enhance interest and participation. Effective promotion is about creating anticipation and making it easy and exciting for people to join in the fun.

By carefully planning and creatively organizing your pickleball socials and mixers, you transform simple gatherings into must-attend events that strengthen the bonds within your community. These events become cherished dates on the calendar, where everyone knows they'll have a fantastic time playing and socializing. So, gather your paddles, pick a theme, and get ready to mix, mingle, and master the art of pickleball socials!

13.3 HOW TO GROW YOUR NETWORK

Building strong partnerships with local businesses, schools, and other organizations can significantly enhance your pickleball club's profile and resource base. Imagine forming a symbiotic relationship with a local sports store that could provide equipment for your tournaments at a discount or as sponsored prizes. Such partnerships bring financial relief and material support and increase your club's visibility within the community. When approaching potential partners, focus on the mutual benefits. For example, local businesses gain exposure to a dedicated community group, enhancing their market presence, while your club enjoys the perks of quality resources and broader recognition. Schools and universities can be approached to facilitate venue sponsorships, where their courts could be used during off-hours, fostering a community connection that encourages students and staff to join in the sport.

Harnessing social media and online platforms can transform the way your pickleball club connects with current and potential members. Platforms like Facebook, Instagram, and Twitter are not just tools for sharing photos and updates; they are powerful engagement engines that can drive event participation and membership growth. Start by creating content that captures pickleball's dynamic nature— action shots from recent matches, video tutorials from your coaches, or testimonials from members about what they love about the club. Engaging content sparks interest and can lead to higher shares and likes, putting your club in front of a broader audience. Managing an online community takes consistency. Regular posts, interactive polls about match times or event preferences, and timely responses to comments and questions keep the community active and engaged. This approach keeps members informed and helps personalize their experience, making them feel genuinely part of the club's family.

Networking with other pickleball clubs and organizations can open new opportunities for your club's members to engage in regional or national events. These connections can be essential for exchanging ideas on club management, member engagement, and event organization. Attend regional meetings, join online forums, and participate in national conferences to connect with other club leaders. Through these interactions, you can draw from the successes and challenges of others, gaining valuable insights to apply to your club's strategies. Additionally, collaborative events or leagues with other clubs enhance the competitive spirit and provide your members with a platform to test their skills against a broader range of players, essential for growth and skill development.

Creating an inclusive and welcoming environment is fundamental to growing your pickleball community. This means actively promoting diversity and ensuring that everyone feels welcome and valued regardless of age, skill level, or background. Simple gestures like offering beginner-friendly sessions, having clear signage and assistance for new members, and hosting social events encouraging mingling can make a big difference. It's also crucial to have policies promoting respect and inclusivity, ensuring that all members have a positive and enriching experience.

Growing your pickleball network through thoughtful partnerships, effective use of digital platforms, strategic networking, and fostering an inclusive community sets a solid foundation for your club's expansion and success. As you implement these strategies, remember that each step forward enhances not just the size of your community but also its quality and cohesion.

Reflection Section

Take a moment to reflect on your club's partnerships and connections. Are there local businesses, educational institutions, or other sports clubs you could forge new relationships with? Consider how enhancing your online presence could engage current and potential members more effectively. What steps can you take this month to create a more inclusive and welcoming environment at your club?

THE FUTURE OF PICKLEBALL

As you look ahead, imagine a world where pickleball adapts to the times and leads the way in sports innovation. This chapter delves into the exciting technological advancements shaping pickleball's future, making it more accessible, enjoyable, and competitive. From smart paddles to virtual reality training systems, the horizon is buzzing with innovations that promise to enhance your pickleball experience. Let's explore how these advancements are changing the game and revolutionizing how we play, train, and connect within the pickleball community.

14.1 TECHNOLOGICAL ADVANCEMENTS

Smart Paddles and Equipment

The evolution of pickleball equipment is leaping forward with the introduction of smart paddles. Imagine a paddle that provides you with real-time data about your performance.

These smart paddles are equipped with sensors that monitor aspects of your play, such as swing speed, ball impact location, and the spin you apply to the ball. Utilizing this technology is like having a coach that provides immediate feedback, allowing you to make adjustments on the fly and refine your techniques with precision.

For instance, if you're consistently hitting the ball too close to the paddle's edge, the sensor can alert you to adjust your swing for better contact. This immediate feedback loop accelerates your learning curve, making practice sessions far more effective. Whether you're a beginner trying to master the basics or an advanced player fine-tuning your skills, smart paddles offer a tailored training experience that adapts to your needs.

Enhanced Court Surfaces

Moving beyond equipment, the surfaces we play on are also getting a makeover. Innovations in court surface materials enhance playability and safety, which is a boon for players of all ages and abilities. New materials are being developed to reduce joint impact, a common concern among players who spend hours on the court. These advanced surfaces are easier on the body and offer improved weather resistance, ensuring a consistent playing experience whether it's a sunny day or a rainy afternoon.

Imagine playing on a surface that blends the perfect amount of grip with cushioning, reducing the risk of slips and falls while easing the strain on your hips, knees, and ankles. These advancements mean you can play longer and recover faster without the lingering aches that might follow a high-intensity game on traditional court surfaces.

Virtual Reality Training Systems

In a world where technology bridges the gap between physical and digital, virtual reality (VR) and augmented reality (AR) systems are transforming how pickleball training is conducted. These systems allow you to practice against virtual opponents, simulating real-game scenarios without needing a physical court. This is especially beneficial if you're looking to practice during off-hours or in locations where pickleball courts are not readily available.

With VR and AR, you can choose different opponents, each programmed with unique styles of play and strategies, providing you with a diverse range of challenges that mimic real-life opponents. Such systems also offer the ability to replay points, analyze your movements, and receive tailored coaching advice based on your performance. It's like having access to a personal pickleball academy right in your living room, providing a convenient and highly effective way to sharpen your skills.

Online Platforms and Mobile Apps

Online platforms and mobile apps are significantly enhancing the community aspect of pickleball. These tools make organizing play, tracking rankings, finding local courts, and connecting with other players easier. Whether you're looking to set up a quick game, join a local tournament, or see where you stand among local players, these platforms offer a wide range of features designed to support your pickleball endeavors.

For example, mobile apps can help you locate the nearest available court, sign up for games or leagues, and even provide route directions. They also serve as social platforms where you can share your progress, celebrate achievements, and connect with fellow pickleball enthusiasts. This integration of technology supports your playing needs and fosters a sense of community, bringing players together both on and off the court.

As you embrace these technological advancements, consider how they can enhance your individual playing experience and contribute to the broader pickleball community. With smart equipment providing personalized feedback, enhanced surfaces offering safer play, virtual training systems allowing for flexible practice, and digital platforms fostering community engagement, the future of the sport looks not just promising but revolutionary. As we continue to explore these innovations, let's remain open to the possibilities they bring, ready to adapt and succeed in this evolving landscape of pickleball.

14.2 INTERNATIONAL GROWTH

Pickleball's charm and accessibility have catapulted it beyond its birthplace in the United States, capturing hearts and sparking competitive spirits around the globe. Now, countries from Canada to Japan and even farther afield in Europe and Asia are embracing this sport with open arms. The global expansion of pickleball is not just about spreading a new sport but also about sharing a culture of fun, fitness, and community. Several factors contribute to its rapid spread and international appeal. For starters, its easy-to-learn nature makes it approachable for all ages and skill levels, breaking down barriers that many other sports face. Additionally, the minimal equipment requirements and the ability to play indoors and outdoors make it adaptable to various settings and climates, further enhancing its global appeal. Countries like Spain and India, with their rich history in racket sports, have seen a natural affinity towards pickleball, with communities quickly forming leagues and tournaments that add a competitive edge to the friendly gameplay.

The surge in international interest has naturally led to increased global competitions, bringing a new level of excitement and professional play to the pickleball community. International tournaments, including world championships and regional competitions, are not just about crowning champions but also about fostering a sense of global community. These events act as melting pots of culture, where players from diverse backgrounds come together, share strategies, and form friendships. The growth of these tournaments is supported by international pickleball federations that work tirelessly to standardize rules and ensure fair play, making the competitions both challenging and rewarding. For instance, the Bainbridge Cup, named after the island where pickleball was invented, now rotates locations across continents, symbolizing the sport's global reach and the shared stewardship of the growing pickleball family.

Pickleball also serves as a vibrant tool for cultural exchange. It's a sport that inherently promotes interaction, where doubles teams with partners from different countries are common and highly encouraged. These cross-cultural teams highlight the sport's unique ability to bridge cultural divides, fostering a deeper understanding and appreciation among its players. Events often feature cultural ceremonies, local cuisine, and language exchanges, turning tournaments into rich cultural experiences. This aspect of pickleball enriches the player's experience and embeds a sense of global citizenship and community among participants.

However, the path to global recognition has its challenges. As pickleball ventures into new territories, it faces hurdles such as variations in access to equipment and facilities. In many parts of the world, finding a dedicated pickleball court is still a rarity, and the availability of quality paddles and balls can be limited, affecting the growth and development of the sport. These challenges, however, open up tremendous opportunities for innovation and investment in the sport. Developing portable, affordable equipment and promoting the construction of modular, multi-use sports facilities could significantly boost pickleball's global footprint. Furthermore, leveraging partnerships with schools and community centers to introduce pickleball could cultivate a new generation of players, ensuring the sport's vibrant future on a global scale.

As pickleball continues to weave its way through different cultures and communities, it promises to bring people together, celebrate diversity, and promote health and wellness on a global scale. This expansion isn't just about playing a game; it's about building a worldwide community that shares in the joy, challenges, and spirit of pickleball.

14.3 EMERGING TRENDS

Innovations in Game Formats

Imagine stepping onto a pickleball court where the rules flex to add zest and challenge to your game, introducing new twists that keep every match exciting and engaging. Innovations in game formats are all about spicing up the pickleball experience, making it more inclusive and varied. For instance, consider time-bound matches, where instead of playing to a specific score, you play within a fixed time limit, say 15 or 20 minutes. This format speeds up the game and introduces a strategic element as players push to score points more aggressively before time runs out, perfect for a quick, intense session when you're short on time.

Another modification could be point-capping rules, where games cap at a certain point regardless of the two-point lead typically required. This change would ensure that every game is tight and competitive, as players near the cap potentially alter their strategies to edge out a win at crucial moments. Mixed-doubles leagues bring an additional layer of diversity, combining different age groups and skill levels. This format promotes a more inclusive environment, allowing seasoned players to mentor younger ones and everyone to learn from diverse playing styles, enriching the community feel of the sport.

These format variations keep the game fresh for long-time enthusiasts and make pickleball more adaptable and appealing to newcomers, ensuring that players of all ages and skill levels can find a format that matches their pace and style. By continuously evolving and experimenting with how pickleball is played, the community ensures that the sport remains vibrant and engaging, attracting a broader audience and keeping the play dynamic and inclusive.

Focus on Youth Engagement

As pickleball continues to captivate hearts, drawing more players into its swift, fun-filled rallies, a particular focus on youth engagement can ensure its vibrant future. Introducing pickleball to younger generations involves strategic outreach and program development, particularly in schools, community centers, and established youth leagues. By integrating pickleball into physical education programs, schools can offer students a fun and accessible way to enhance their physical fitness, coordination, and team-building skills. The simplicity and quick learning curve of pickleball make it an ideal addition to school curriculums, engaging students in a physical activity that is both enjoyable and socially enriching.

Community centers and local sports clubs can host youth leagues or summer camps focusing on pickleball, providing structured play and instruction catering to young enthusiasts. These programs boost skill development and physical fitness and cultivate a sense of community and belonging among participants, encouraging healthy lifestyle habits and team-work. Moreover, pickleball events for families and young players can include mini-tournaments, family play days, and skills clinics, making the sport a staple in community recreation offerings.

These initiatives cultivate a new generation of pickleball players and embed the sport deeper into the community fabric, ensuring its growth and sustainability. Engaging youth not only secures the future of pickleball but also enriches the lives of young players with valuable life skills learned on the court.

Sustainability Practices in Pickleball

As awareness of environmental impact grows, the world of sports is no exception, and pickleball is stepping up to the challenge. Embracing sustainability within pickleball involves several facets, from eco-friendly equipment and apparel to developing green facilities. Manufacturers are increasingly exploring sustainable materials for paddles and balls, reducing the reliance on non-renewable resources and minimizing waste. Apparel made from recycled materials or designed for extended durability contributes to a more sustainable practice, reducing the environmental footprint associated with frequent replacement and disposal.

Moreover, the construction of pickleball facilities is seeing innovations such as using recycled materials, energy-efficient lighting, and water-conserving landscapes. These green facilities lower the ecological impact and create healthier environments for players, promoting well-being through clean air and natural settings. By prioritizing sustainability, the pickleball community enhances its appeal to environmentally conscious players and contributes to broader ecological health, setting a positive example in the sports world.

Health and Wellness Integration

Pickleball's potential extends beyond just being a sport; it's a vehicle for promoting health and wellness, especially among aging populations. Integrating pickleball into health and wellness programs involves partnerships with health organizations, wellness retreats, and rehabilitation centers, where pickleball is used as a therapeutic and fitness tool. For seniors, pickleball offers a low-impact alternative to more strenuous activities, allowing them to maintain physical activity without over-straining joints, which is crucial for mobility and cardiovascular health.

Wellness retreats can incorporate pickleball into their offerings, providing fun, community-building exercise options that complement traditional wellness activities like yoga and meditation. In rehabilitation settings, pickleball can aid in recovery and therapy, helping patients improve their motor skills, balance, and coordination in an enjoyable, social environment. These integrations make pickleball a holistic tool for enhancing physical health and mental well-being, enriching lives through active, communal play.

As pickleball continues to evolve and expand, embracing these trends will enrich the sport and reinforce its role as a catalyst for health, community, and environmental stewardship. Looking forward, integrating innovative game formats, youth engagement strategies, sustainability practices, and health and wellness initiatives will ensure that pickleball remains a beloved, dynamic, and positive force in the lives of players worldwide. Now, let's turn the page to explore how you can take these insights and apply them directly in your next game.

LIFESTYLE BENEFITS

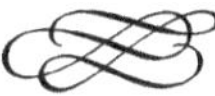

Imagine pickleball not just as a sport but as a vibrant thread woven seamlessly into the fabric of your daily life. It's more than a game; it's a lifestyle that blends excitement, health, and community while respecting the balance of your everyday responsibilities. Whether you're a student juggling classes, a professional balancing work demands, or a parent managing a household, integrating pickleball into your busy schedule can seem challenging but incredibly rewarding. Let's explore how you can make pickleball a harmonious part of your life, ensuring it enriches rather than complicates your daily routine.

15.1 LIFE BALANCE

Prioritizing Time Management

In today's fast-paced world, finding time for activities like pickleball can often feel like trying to solve a complex puzzle. However, with some strategic planning, you can fit pickleball into your schedule without overwhelming yourself. Start by identifying typically free times in your week. Early mornings, lunch breaks, or weekend afternoons can be golden opportunities for a quick game. Utilizing calendar apps can be a game-changer here. Try blocking out specific times for pickleball just as you would for a meeting or a doctor's appointment. This not only commits you to play but also ensures others know you're unavailable during these times.

Combining pickleball sessions with other daily activities can also maximize your time. For instance, if you're heading out for a family day in the park, bring your pickleball gear along. You can enjoy a few rounds while the kids play, or your partner reads a book. Similarly, consider scheduling games during your lunch break if your workplace is near a court. It's a fantastic way to break up the workday, re-energize, and return to your duties with a refreshed mind.

Communicating with Family and Employers

For many, the challenge isn't finding time—it's justifying it to others. Communicating the value of sport to those who don't play—be it family or employers—is crucial. Explain how playing pickleball is not merely about the sport but also about maintaining health, reducing stress, and nurturing social connections, ultimately making you a happier, more balanced person. For family, highlight how it enhances quality time together, whether they join you on the court or support you from the sidelines. For employers, underscore how taking a brief break for physical activity can boost productivity and creativity. If possible, invite them to join a game; experiencing the joys of pickleball firsthand can turn skeptics into supporters.

Setting Realistic Goals

Setting goals is a highly effective tool for motivating and guiding your pickleball involvement. When setting goals, consider what is realistically achievable within your current lifestyle. It could be as simple as playing once a week, participating in a local league, or attending a specific tournament annually. Make sure these goals are flexible; life's unpredictabilities mean sometimes adjustments are necessary. Treat your goals as guides, not ultimatums, allowing yourself the flexibility to shift priorities as needed without feeling guilty.

Balancing Competitive and Recreational Play

Pickleball offers a spectrum of play, from highly competitive tournaments to casual weekend games. Finding the right balance can significantly affect your enjoyment and stress levels. If competition brings you joy and invigorates you, by all means, explore tournaments and competitive leagues. However, if you find these settings stressful, focus on the recreational side of pickleball. Playing for fun with friends or family, without the pressure of scores and stakes, can be just as fulfilling. Many find that competing when they feel up to the challenge and playing recreationally when they need a relaxed, joyful escape helps maintain a healthy, happy equilibrium.

Incorporating pickleball into your life shouldn't feel like a chore or another box to tick on your to-do list. It's about weaving this activity into your every day, finding joy in the rallies, and cherishing the community it builds. By managing your time wisely, communicating its value to those around you, setting achievable goals, and balancing the competitive with the recreational, pickleball becomes not just a game you play, but a significant, enriching part of your life.

15.2 FAMILY TIME

Pickleball is a fantastic way to unite the family, offering a unique mix of fun, physical activity, and the chance to bond over a shared interest. Introducing your family to pickleball can be a joyful experience, especially when you approach it with the right mindset and preparation. The key is to make the first experience as enjoyable and stress-free as possible. Start with simplified rules to keep it easy and engaging. For younger children or those new to racket sports, consider modifying the game by reducing the scoring complexity or allowing a bounce in the non-volley zone. Mini-games are also an excellent way to introduce the sport. You could set up fun challenges like 'hit the target, where different zones on the court have points, or 'keep it up,'" where the goal is to volley the ball as many times as possible without letting it hit the ground. These games keep the atmosphere light and playful, perfect for a family setting.

When planning a family pickleball outing, choosing the right location is crucial. Look for local courts that are family-friendly, with safe, well-maintained facilities. Many community centers and parks have pickleball courts open to the public and are often less crowded during off-peak hours, which can be ideal for families. Make sure to bring the appropriate equipment for everyone, including paddles of various sizes for children and adults and lighter balls that are easier for beginners to handle. It's also a good idea to pack plenty of water, snacks, and a picnic to enjoy after the games. To make the day more enjoyable, consider incorporating activities such as frisbee, tag, or a simple walk in the park, allowing everyone to have fun and relax together.

Setting up friendly family competitions can really spice up your pickleball play. Organize a mini-tournament or ladder match where each family member competes against all others to climb the "family pickleball ladder." You can create teams for doubles matches, which helps balance the skill levels and promotes teamwork. Keep track of everyone's scores and progress on a leaderboard to add a fun and competitive element. Awarding small prizes or certificates can also be a great motivator. These friendly competitions can become a cherished family tradition, creating lasting memories and friendly rivalry everyone looks forward to.

Pickleball also presents an excellent opportunity to teach valuable life skills. For children and adults alike, the game can reinforce the importance of sportsmanship—learning to win gracefully and lose with dignity. Team play and doubles can teach coordination and cooperation, showing that working effectively with others can lead to greater success. The physical aspects of the game improve fitness, coordination, and agility, promoting a healthy lifestyle. Moreover, the strategic nature of pickleball encourages problem-solving and quick thinking, skills that are beneficial both on and off the court.

As the day winds down and the paddles are put away, the echoes of laughter and the joy of a day spent together linger. This chapter isn't just about playing pickleball; it's about weaving it into the fabric of family life, where every serve and volley brings you closer. Through thoughtful introduction, well-planned outings, spirited competitions, and the lessons interwoven in the game, pickleball becomes more than a sport —it becomes a vehicle for bonding, learning, and making memories that enrich your family's life.

As we wrap up this chapter, remember that integrating pickleball into your family isn't just about the hours spent on the court. It's about the smiles, the high-fives, and the shared joy that each game brings, strengthening bonds and creating a shared family legacy of health, happiness, and togetherness.

CONCLUSION

Wow, what a journey we've embarked on together! From grasping the fundamentals to exploring advanced strategies that can elevate your game, we hope this book has equipped you with the skills you need and sparked a lasting passion for pickleball. As we wrap up, let's look at how you can continue to grow, connect, and integrate this fantastic sport into every facet of your life.

SETTING NEW CHALLENGES AND GOALS

As you progress on your pickleball journey, setting new challenges and goals is essential to keep your motivation high and skills sharp. Whether aiming to improve your serve accuracy, stepping up to higher-level tournaments, or even mastering a tricky new shot, always have a goal in mind. Remember, goals are personal. What matters is that they push you a little further, helping you grow not just as a player but as a person, too.

DIVERSIFYING PICKLEBALL ACTIVITIES

Pickleball is more than just a game; it's a gateway to endless fun and learning opportunities. Why not mix things up a bit? Attend a workshop to refine your techniques or learn from the pros. Try out different playing formats—perhaps a doubles game if you usually play singles or join a pickleball league. Exploring new venues can also add a fresh twist to your game. Each new court brings its own set of challenges and opportunities to learn, making your pickleball experience continually exciting.

CONNECTING WITH THE PICKLEBALL COMMUNITY

One of the most rewarding aspects of pickleball is the vibrant community that comes with it. Engage with other pickleball enthusiasts through social media, join local clubs, or become a member of national organizations. Volunteering at pickleball events or contributing to related charities can also be a deeply rewarding way to give back to the community that supports your passion. These connections offer not just camaraderie and support but also a wealth of knowledge and experience that can help you improve your game. Participating in community activities enriches your pickleball experience, giving you a sense of belonging and shared passion that goes beyond the court.

As we close this chapter together, remember that every game of pickleball, much like every page of this book, is a step forward in your journey. Keep playing, learning, and, most importantly, enjoying every moment on the court. Here's to countless more games filled with laughter, learning, and the love of pickleball. Thank you for sharing this journey with us. Now, go out there and make every shot count!

MAKE A DIFFERENCE WITH YOUR REVIEW

UNLOCK THE POWER OF GENEROSITY

"Small acts, when multiplied by millions of people, can transform the world."

— HOWARD ZINN

People who help others without expecting anything in return often lead happier, longer lives. That's why I'm asking for your help with something simple but powerful.

Would you lend a hand to someone you've never met, even if you never get credit for it?

Who is this person? They're someone like you—curious about pickleball, eager to learn, and looking for the right guidance.

Our mission with *Pickleball for Everyone* is to make pickleball accessible to all. Whether you're new to the game or refining your skills, this book is designed for everyone, including players with disabilities. But to truly reach everyone, we need a little help.

This is where you come in. Many people judge a book by its reviews. So, here's my request on behalf of a pickleball enthusiast you've never met:

Please help that future player by leaving a review for this book.

Your review costs nothing and takes less than 60 seconds, but it can make a huge difference. Your feedback could help...

...one more person discover the joy of pickleball.

...one more beginner find the confidence to join a game.

...one more player feel included and supported.

To make a real impact and help someone discover the world of pickleball, all you have to do is leave a review.

Simply scan the QR code below to leave your review:

[https://www.amazon.com/review/review-your-purchases/?asin=BOOKASIN]

If you feel good about helping a fellow pickleball player, you're exactly the kind of person this community needs. Welcome to the team!

Thank you from the bottom of our heart. Now, let's keep enjoying the game we love.

- Your biggest fan, Atwater Publishing

PS: When you share what you love with others, you help them grow. If you think this book could help another pickleball enthusiast, pass it along and keep the passion alive.

REFERENCES

Selkirk. (n.d.). **How to keep score in pickleball: A beginner's guide**. Retrieved from https://www.selkirk.com/blogs/pickleball-education/how-to-keep-score-in-pickleball-a-beginners-guide

Pickleball.si. (n.d.). **Pickleball Equipment: A Guide to Paddles, Balls, and Nets**. Retrieved from https://pickleball.si.com/guides/pickleball-equipment-a-guide-to-paddles-balls-and-nets

USA Pickleball. (n.d.). **Adaptive / Wheelchair Pickleball**. Retrieved from https://usapickleball.org/play/wheelchair-pickleball/

Recess Pickleball. (n.d.). **Understanding the Pickleball Court: A Comprehensive Guide**. Retrieved from https://www.recesspickleball.com/blogs/pickleball/mastering-the-pickleball-court-a-comprehensive-guide-to-court-dimensions

Pickleball Central. (n.d.). **Pickleball Serve 101: The Ultimate Beginner's Guide**. Retrieved from https://www.youtube.com/watch?v=gpoifV4-xdk

Paddletek. (n.d.). **9 Tips to Improve Pickleball Volleys**. Retrieved from https://www.paddletek.com/blogs/news/better-pickleball-volleys

Cole, B. (n.d.). **Pickleball Drills and Exercises: Improving Your Skills and Performance**. Retrieved from https://www.briancolemd.com/blog-post/sports/pickleball-drills-and-exercises-improving-your-skills-and-performance/

Pickleball Union. (n.d.). **11 Game-Winning Pickleball Tips For Intermediate Players**. Retrieved from https://pickleballunion.com/pickleball-tips-for-intermediate-players/

Pickleball University. (n.d.). **The Best Pickleball Drills To Improve Your 3rd Shot Drop**. Retrieved from https://www.pickleballuniversity.com/home/the-best-pickleball-drills-to-improve-your-3rd-shot-drop

Luxe Pickleball. (n.d.). **Offensive and Defensive Strategies in Pickleball**. Retrieved from https://luxepickleball.com/blogs/news/mastering-the-transition-offensive-and-defensive-strategies-in-pickleball

AbilityX. (n.d.). **Adaptive Sports Gear for Athletes with Disabilities**. Retrieved from https://abilityx.io/news/adaptive-sports-gear-for-athletes-with-disabilities-find-your-perfect-fit/

National Institutes of Health. (n.d.). **Benefits of Adaptive Sport on Physical and Mental Quality**. Retrieved from https://www.ncbi.nlm.nih.gov/pmc/articles/PMC10531072/

Inclusive Sport Design. (n.d.). **How to Adapt and Modify Your Sport Activities to Include All**. Retrieved from https://www.inclusivesportdesign.com/blog-posts/how-to-adapt-and-modify-your-sport-activities-to-include-all

Life Time. (n.d.). **Pickleball Is for Kids, Too! How to Get Them Started**. Retrieved from https://experiencelife.lifetime.life/article/pickleball-is-for-kids-too-how-to-get-them-started/

USA Pickleball. (n.d.). **Health & Safety**. Retrieved from https://usapickleball.org/play/health-safety/

TicketSource. (n.d.). **How To Plan And Organise A Sports Event In 14 Steps**. Retrieved from https://www.ticketsource.us/blog/how-to-plan-a-sport-event

American Association of Adapted Sports Programs. (n.d.). **Home**. Retrieved from https://adaptedsports.org/

Tennis Fitness. (n.d.). **Pickleball Workout Plan | Strength and Conditioning**. Retrieved from https://www.tennisfitness.com/blog/ultimate-pickleball-workout-plan

EW Motion Therapy. (n.d.). **Eight Common Pickleball Injuries and How To Prevent Them**. Retrieved from https://www.ewmotiontherapy.com/blog/common-pickleball-injuries-prevent

USTA. (n.d.). **Dynamic Warm-up and Flexibility Training for Tennis**. Retrieved from https://www.usta.com/en/home/improve/tips-and-instruction/national/dynamic-warm-up-and-flexibility-training.html

Challenged Athletes Foundation. (n.d.). **Adaptive Sports Equipment**. Retrieved from https://www.challengedathletes.org/adaptive-equipment/

Red Bull. (n.d.). **Mental Toughness in Athletes: How to Develop Grit**. Retrieved from https://www.redbull.com/us-en/mental-toughness-athletes-grit

Verywell Fit. (n.d.). **How Imagery and Visualization Can Improve Athletic Performance**. Retrieved from https://www.verywellfit.com/visualization-techniques-for-athletes-3119438

Blayze. (n.d.). **Science of Breath Work: Breathing for Athletes**. Retrieved from https://blayze.io/blog/general/the-science-of-breathing-for-athletes

Newport Institute. (n.d.). **Building Resilience Through Sports**. Retrieved from https://www.newportinstitute.com/resources/mental-health/building-mental-resilience/

The Pickler. (n.d.). **6 Pickleball Rule Changes to Learn for 2023**. Retrieved from https://thepickler.com/pickleball-blog/2023-pickleball-rule-changes/

Medium. (n.d.). **How Technology is Revolutionizing Pickleball Equipment**. Retrieved from https://medium.com/@pickleballbynova/pioneering-the-future-how-technology-is-revolutionizing-pickleball-equip-ment-ee5b1a5270bb

USA Pickleball. (n.d.). **Pickleball Annual Growth Report**. Retrieved from [https://usapickleball.org/about-us/organizational-docs/pickleball-annual-growth-report/](https://usapickleball.org/about-us/organiza tional-doc